VIKING SOCIETY FOR NORTHERN RESEARCH
TEXT SERIES

GENERAL EDITORS

Anthony Faulkes and Richard Perkins

VOLUME X

ÁGRIP AF NÓREGSKONUNGASǪGUM

ÁGRIP AF NÓREGSKONUNGASǪGUM

A TWELFTH-CENTURY SYNOPTIC HISTORY OF THE KINGS OF NORWAY

EDITED AND TRANSLATED
WITH AN INTRODUCTION AND NOTES

BY

M. J. DRISCOLL

SECOND EDITION

VIKING SOCIETY FOR NORTHERN RESEARCH
UNIVERSITY COLLEGE LONDON
2008

Bók þessi er tileinkuð vinum mínum á Árnastofnun

© Matthew James Driscoll 1995
Second edition with corrections and additions 2008
Reprinted 2020

ISBN: 978 0 903521 75 8

The cover illustration is based on a figure attached to the shrine of St Manchan, Boher, County Offaly, which was probably made in Ireland in the twelfth century. It is thought to represent St Óláfr.

The maps are based on those in *Íslenzk fornrit* XXIX by permission of Hið íslenzka fornritafélag

Printed by
Short Run Press Limited, Exeter

CONTENTS

Acknowledgments vi
Preface to second edition vii
Introduction ix
    (i)   Manuscript and provenance ix
    (ii) *Ágrip*'s sources xiii
    (iii) Style and language xviii
    Editorial principles xx
    (i)   Orthography and morphology xx
    (ii) Punctuation, chapter division etc. xxiii
    (iii) Previous editions and translations xxiv
    A note on the translation xxv
Text and translation 1
Notes to the translation 82
Bibliography and abbreviations 109
Index of personal names 116
Index of place-names 120
Index of other names 126

Illustrations

Facsimile of folio 5v of the manuscript viii
Map of Denmark 121
Map of Central and South Norway 122–23
Map of Sweden and the Baltic 124

Acknowledgments

The present work began life as a BA dissertation, or 'Semester 8 project', in English Studies at the University of Stirling, Scotland, completed in the spring of 1979. The Viking Society agreed to publish it fairly quickly thereafter, but one thing or another has prevented its publication until now. Owing to the work's long gestation period, there are a great many people to whom I owe my thanks. Ursula Dronke first suggested the idea of a translation with commentary of *Ágrip* and Michael Alexander, now Professor of English at St Andrews, supervised the original project. I edited the text from photographs of the manuscript at Stofnun Árna Magnússonar in Reykjavík, checking my text subsequently against the manuscript itself at Det Arnamagnæanske Institut in Copenhagen; to the staffs of both these institutions I owe my gratitude, in particular to Ólafur Halldórsson and Stefán Karlsson in Reykjavík and to Jonna Louis-Jensen in Copenhagen. I should also like to acknowledge the help of Christopher Sanders of Den arnamagnæanske kommissions ordbog. Others who have helped in one way or another in the preparation of this volume include Bjarni Einarsson, who very kindly read over my introduction and notes at an early stage and made available to me the text of his edition while it was still in proof, Bjarni Guðnason, who read over the first draft of my text, and Carolyne Larrington, who also read over the notes and made a number of valuable comments and suggestions. Anthony Faulkes and Richard Perkins have both read over the entire work, the former probably more times than he would care to remember, and to both of them I owe a debt of gratitude. Finally, I should like to thank my wife Ragnheiður, without whose help and encouragement I should probably never have completed this—or indeed any other—project. It is a sobering thought that at no time during our married life have I not, in theory at least, been working on *Ágrip*.

M. J. Driscoll
Reykjavík
September 1994

Preface to second edition

For this reprint I have taken the opportunity to correct some errors and infelicities in the first printing, among them several brought to my attention in reviews of the book, in particular those by Jan Ragnar Hagland (*Maal og Minne* 2 (1996), 215–16) and Kari Ellen Gade (*Alvíssmál* 7 (1997), 112–15). Hallgrímur J. Ámundason's MA thesis from 2001, an edition of *Ágrip* with detailed palaeographic and linguistic commentary, has also prompted me to revise a number of readings in my own edition. I have not, however, made substantial revisions to the introduction (except in section (i)) or notes, nor have I updated the bibliography.

M. J. Driscoll
Copenhagen
May 2007

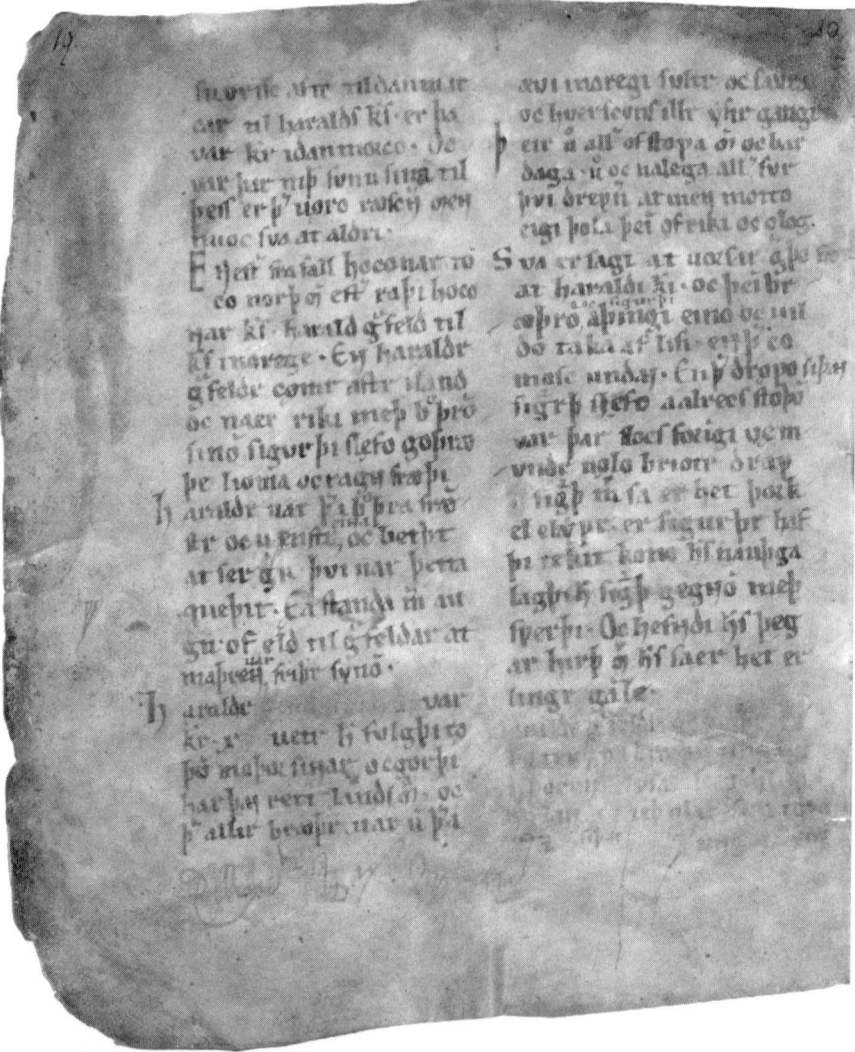

AM 325 II 4to, folio 5v (see pp. 16 and 18)
Photo: Suzanne Reitz, Den Arnamagnæanske Samling, Copenhagen

INTRODUCTION

(i) *Manuscript and provenance*

Ágrip af Nóregskonungasǫgum, or simply *Ágrip*, is the name given by modern scholars[1] to a short text, written in the vernacular, dealing with the history of the kings of Norway from the late ninth to the early twelfth century, and preserved in a single Icelandic manuscript, AM 325 II 4to, dating from the first half of the thirteenth century.[2] The manuscript is imperfect, comprising in its present form four quires, the first, second and fourth of them originally consisting of eight leaves, the third of seven. The first leaf of the first quire was at some point cut from the rest, so that nothing remains of it apart from a strip 1.5 cm wide along the inner margin. In addition, only two leaves, a bifolium, remain of the fourth quire, with the result that there are two significant lacunae toward the end of the text. A fifth quire generally assumed to have followed has left no trace. The text is written in two columns throughout, which is rather unusual for a small quarto manuscript (*c*.15 × 13 cm), most of 25 lines. There are two contemporary hands, otherwise unknown, but clearly those of practised scribes. The first of these writes fols 1r–22v, i. e. to the end of chapter LV in the present edition, and the second fols 23 and 24. Some scholars have argued for a third hand on fol. 24, but the evidence for this is insubstantial.[3] Spaces for initials and chapter headings were left by the scribes but not filled in. A later, probably fifteenth-century, hand has added initials and chapter headings in greenish-coloured ink on fols 8r, 8v, 9r, 10r and 11r. Although the

---

[1] The name derives from Finnur Magnússon's edition in *Fornmanna sögur* X, 'Stutt ágrip af Noregs konúnga sögum' ('Short summary of the histories of the kings of Norway'), which was in turn probably suggested by Árni Magnússon's description of the text, 'Compendium Historiæ Norvegicæ'; see *Katalog* 1889–94, I 553.

[2] *Katalog* 1889–94, I 553; cf. *Ágrip* 1880, xxxiv. Hreinn Benediktsson 1965, xxi, gives the date more specifically as 'probably towards the middle of the first half of the 13th century'. Munch (*Ágrip* 1834, 273) initially declared the manuscript to be from the fourteenth century, but later (Oddr Snorrason 1853, vi) referred to it as 'et . . . Haandskrift, der neppe kan være stort yngre end 1200'; Konráð Gíslason (1846, xxxviii) dated it to the early thirteenth century, and similar datings—late twelfth or early thirteenth century—are found in Storm (1871, 414: 'ved Aar 1200 eller lidt senere'), Bugge (1873, 2: 'rimelig ikke længe efter 1200') and Guðbrandur Vigfússon (1878, lxxxvii: 'end of the twelfth century').

[3] E. g. Dahlerup (*Ágrip* 1880, xxvii–xxx) and Hreinn Benediktsson (1965, xxi); cf. Brieskorn 1909, 149–52; Finnur Jónsson, *Ágrip* 1929, viii.

ink has faded somewhat most of these chapters headings can still be made out, e.g. fol. 8rb 'floti astridar' ('Ástríðr's flight'), fol. 9rb 'vm olaf konung' ('Concerning King Óláfr') and fol. 10ra 'Gipting olafs konungs' ('The marriage of King Óláfr'). There are, in addition to these, several marginal notes in later hands. On fol. 4v, for example, the words 'hialmadr og brynjadr' ('helmeted and mail-clad') are written in a fifteenth-century hand, imitating an addition made to the text by the scribe at this point (cf. p. 14 note b). Probably in the same hand is a comment in the lower margin of fol. 5r: 'þetta þiki mer vera gott blek ennda kann ek icki b[e]tr[a] sia' ('this seems to me to be good ink, at least as far as I can see'), presumably a pen trial. In the bottom margin of fol. 9v a rather amateurish hand, probably of the seventeenth century, has written: 'þessa bok uilda eg gæt lært meda[n] Gud gefe myer Gott ad læra' ('I would like to study this book while God makes it possible for me to study'). There are also illegible scribbles in a later hand (or hands) on fols 2r, 3r, 5v, 6r and 19r. On fol. 16r a similar hand has written what appears to be the name 'Þorgeir Jónsson'; this is presumably Þorgeir Jónsson (c.1661–1742), brother of Bishop Steinn Jónsson and *ráðsmaður* (steward) at Hólar, one of the manuscript's previous owners.[4]

One unusual aspect of the manuscript is the very large number of erasures. Throughout the manuscript single words, groups of words and even whole sentences have been erased, often so thoroughly that it is now impossible to see what had been written there. In a few cases these may be the work of the scribe himself—in one instance at least a scribal error has clearly been corrected—but as the spaces have for the most part been left empty this is unlikely to be true for the majority. Four lines at the end of chapter IX have been erased, presumably because the same events are dealt with more fully later in the book and someone, perhaps the scribe himself, wanted to avoid the repetition, but for most of the erasures there is no apparent reason. Curiously, few of them in any way affect the grammar or syntax. It is, suggests Bjarni Einarsson, as if someone had, as a kind of diversion, gone through the manuscript looking for words that could be removed without damaging the text.[5]

Ágrip's forty-eight pages span the period of Norway's history from the death of Hálfdan svarti ('the black') in about 880 to the accession of Ingi krókhryggr ('the hunchback') in 1136. In its original form, however, the text is thought to have begun with Hálfdan's reign and

---

[4] For a full description of the manuscript see *Ágrip* 1880, iii–vi.
[5] *Ágrip* 1984, vi.

continued, like the more expansive and better-known series of Kings' Sagas *Heimskringla* and *Fagrskinna*, down to the accession of Sverrir Sigurðarson in 1177.[6]

Several features of the text—omissions, dittographies etc., and the fact that there is more than one hand—indicate that it must be a copy of an older original. Some scholars have suggested that even when complete the extant version represented no more than an abridgement of a much longer text.[7] Most agree that although the manuscript itself is without doubt Icelandic,[8] the original must certainly have been written in Norway.[9] That the author was Norwegian—or at least writing in Norway[10]—is suggested by a number of factors. The orthography of the manuscript is inconsistent and in many respects quite odd, and at least some of the features it exhibits must be due to a Norwegian exemplar.[11] There are also several anomalous morphological forms, some of which are clear 'Norwegianisms', and many of the nicknames used in *Ágrip*—*háfœta* ('high-leg'), *hvítbeinn* ('white-leg'), *lafskegg* ('dangling beard'), *berleggr* ('bare-leg')—are different from those normally found in Icelandic sources, and may therefore represent Norwegian, rather than Icelandic, tradition.[12]

---

[6] See e. g. *Ágrip* 1984, xvii; Indrebø 1922, 19. Maurer (1867, 146) thought it to have continued down to 1161, and Dahlerup (*Ágrip* 1880, iii) that it 'har sluttet med Sigurd Jorsalefarer', i. e. in 1130 (like Theodoricus).

[7] E. g. Guðbrandur Vigfússon 1878, lxxxvii: 'As the only example of an *Icelandic* abridgement it is interesting.' Much of the evidence for this view is discussed by Sigurður Nordal (1914, 46–48).

[8] See e. g. Konráð Gíslason 1846, xxxviii.

[9] Icelandic provenance has occasionally been claimed; see e. g. Jón Þorkelsson 1856, 141–42 and 147–48 ('getum vèr eigi sèð, að það sè nein sönnun fyrir norskum uppruna . . . Ágrips af Noregs konunga sögum'). More recently, Bjarni Guðnason (1977, 119) has been content to say merely that 'Ágrip er ef til vill íslenskt að uppruna'.

[10] Finnur Jónsson 1920–24, II 618–19, claims that while *Ágrip* may well have been written in Norway, 'må det betragtes som utvivlsomt, at forfatteren er en Islænder'. The argument is wonderfully circular: no Norwegian is known to have written a historical text in the vernacular—after all, Sverrir and Hákon Hákonarson both imported Icelanders to write their sagas—ergo, no historical text in the vernacular can have been written by a Norwegian.

[11] On 'Norwegianisms' in the text see *Ágrip* 1880, xxx–xxxiii; Storm 1873, 25–27; and Hægstad 1906–42, II.2, 156; see also, however, *Ágrip* 1929, ix. Generally, care must be taken when assessing the value of such 'Norwegianisms', as their presence in Icelandic manuscripts does not in any way demonstrate Norwegian origin; see Stefán Karlsson 1978 and 1979.

[12] See Indrebø 1922, 56–57.

The text itself provides some information on its author. Unlike saga-authors generally, the author of Ágrip evinces little interest in, and indeed some ignorance of, Iceland and Icelanders.[13] He misinterprets a kenning in one of the skaldic verses he cites, which, it has been claimed, no 'educated Icelander of that day' could have done.[14] The centre of much of the action is Niðaróss (modern Trondheim), which is often referred to simply as Kaupangr ('town'), and with which the reader is apparently expected to be familiar. The Þrœndir—the people of Þrándheimr, the modern-day Trøndelag—are mentioned five times in the text, as against only one mention each for the inhabitants of other parts of the country, the Vǫrsar, Upplendingar, Háleygir and Mœrir, suggesting that the author's interests were centred there, and that he himself may have lived there, and there have written his book.

One might also be forgiven for detecting in Ágrip an underlying Norwegian national sentiment, particularly with regard to its presentation of the various achievements of the Norwegian royal house. In chapter XLIX, for example, Magnús berfœttr's expedition to Sweden (in Heimskringla and in foreign chronicles a Norwegian defeat) is presented as a resounding victory.

It is also possible to discern in Ágrip a certain tendentiousness. The author, obviously a cleric, clearly sides with Ingi krókhryggr and his follower Gregóríús Dagsson, which would suggest that he was an opponent of the Birkibeinar, or 'Birch-legs', and that his work was, at least in part, polemical, intended to convince the populace that the descendants of the kings who had collaborated with the church were more worthy of their support than the Birkibeinar and their followers.[15]

Discernible also is a tendency on the part of the author to take the part of 'the people'—lýðrinn, a word occurring with unusual frequency in the text—against bad kings who impose taxes and hardships.[16] Ágrip is decidedly not an aristocratic work.

Ágrip is generally said to have been written 'c.1190'.[17] This date has been arrived at because Ágrip's author, as we shall see below, is thought to have made use of another Norwegian synoptic history, Historia de antiquitate regum Norwagiensium, written by one

[13] Indrebø 1922, 58–59.
[14] Turville-Petre 1953, 173; see note 9 to the translation below, pp. 83–84.
[15] See Paasche 1922. An account of the background to this dispute can be found in Gathorne-Hardy 1956.
[16] See Indrebø 1922, 43–45.
[17] See e. g. Ágrip 1984, x–xi.

'Theodoricus monachus', which, on the basis of internal evidence, would appear to have been written shortly after 1177 but certainly before 1188,[18] thus providing us with a convenient *terminus post quem* for *Ágrip*. The only certain *terminus ante quem* is the date of the manuscript itself, i. e. the first half of the thirteenth century, as was said above, but there is some external evidence (not, admittedly, a great deal) to indicate that it is somewhat older than that. Snorri Sturluson knew *Ágrip*, and used it in his *Heimskringla*, thought to have been written around 1230. *Fagrskinna* and the so-called 'Legendary saga' of Óláfr Haraldsson, both of which predate *Heimskringla*, appear also to have used *Ágrip*, pushing its likely date of composition back somewhat further. Finally, certain similarities between passages in *Ágrip* and in the Icelandic translation of Oddr Snorrason's *Óláfs saga Tryggvasonar*, thought to date from about 1200, suggest that *Ágrip* was known to the translator.[19] If so, *Ágrip* must have been written sometime before 1200 but after 1188, hence '*c*.1190'.

(ii) *Ágrip's sources*

'The history of Icelandic literature', wrote Jón Helgason, 'contains no more intricate problem than that of the relationship between the various Sagas about the Norwegian Kings.'[20] Scholarship on the Kings' Sagas has in general tended to concentrate on this question of sources and textual relations, often to the exclusion of all else, so that one may occasionally find oneself in agreement with Theodore M. Andersson's recent comment that 'the charm of kings' saga study is decidedly remote'.[21]

Ágrip lies in many ways at the very heart of the 'problem' of the Kings' Sagas. While its influence on subsequent material is fairly clear—it became known in Iceland soon after its composition and was used, as was mentioned above, by Snorri in his *Heimskringla*—the nature of the sources used by the author of *Ágrip* himself has been the subject of much learned debate over the last century and a half, particularly as regards *Ágrip*'s relationship to the two other Norwegian synoptic histories, Theodoricus's *Historia de Antiquitate Regum Norwagiensium* and the anonymous *Historia Norvegiæ*.[22]

---

[18] Nordal 1914, 8–9.
[19] See Bjarni Aðalbjarnarson 1937, 57–58; Nordal 1914, 37–39.
[20] 1934, 12.
[21] 1985, 198.
[22] See Ulset 1983, 16–47.

Theodoricus's book, written in Latin, begins with the reign of Haraldr hárfagri and ends with the death of Sigurðr Jórsalafari in 1130, and must have been composed, as noted above, sometime between 1177 and 1188. Despite a number of attempts to do so, it does not seem possible to pin-point the date of composition within that period,[23] although it is customary to see it as nearer the beginning of the period than the end.[24] Theodoricus's sources have, like *Ágrip*'s, been the subject of much debate. He himself says that he has based his account on the reports, therefore presumably oral, of Icelanders, who know more about these things than anyone else, having preserved these stories in their poetry.[25] Although he appears to claim to have had no written sources—he is reporting, he stresses, what he has heard, not seen ('non visa sed audita')—he refers in the text to a *Catalogus regum norwagiensium*, presumably a written work,[26] and he seems also to have known a *Translatio S. Olavi*.[27] Neither of these has survived.

Historia Norvegiæ, also written in Latin, is preserved in a single fragmentary manuscript containing texts and documents in Latin and Scots relating to the history of Orkney, Scotland and Norway. P. A. Munch, the first editor of the *Historia Norvegiæ*,[28] considered the manuscript to be Orcadian and to date from the mid-fifteenth century, but Michael Chesnutt has demonstrated that it cannot have been compiled before 1500, and then on the Scottish mainland.[29] The original is thought to have been Norwegian. Little can be said with any certainty with regard to its date of composition, but various scholars have suggested dates ranging from 1152–63 to 1266 or later.[30] In its present

---

[23] See Lange 1989, 20–22.

[24] See e. g. Nordal 1914, 8–9.

[25] 'Operæ pretium duxi . . . pauca hæc de antiquitate regum Norwagiensium breviter annotare, et prout sagaciter perquirere potuimus ab eis, penes quos horum memoria præcipue vigere creditur, quos nos Islendinga vocamus, qui hæc in suis antiquis carminibus percelebrata recolunt.' (*MHN* 3)

[26] See Ellehøj 1965, 182–96.

[27] The *Translatio* is discussed in e. g. *MHN* xxxiv; Nordal 1914, 10–12; Bjarni Aðalbjarnarson 1937, 6; Jónas Kristjánsson 1972, 146–47.

[28] *Symbolæ ad historiam antiquiorem Norvegicarum* (1850).

[29] Chesnutt 1985.

[30] Hanssen (1949, 28) dated it to 1152–63; Storm (*MHN* xxiii) suggested 1180–90; Koht (1919, 102; 1921, 211–13), Schreiner (1928, 73) and Ellehøj (1965, 144–46; 295), favoured *c.*1170; Finnur Jónsson (1920–24, II 594; 1928, 276), Paasche (1957, 464–65) and Bjarni Aðalbjarnarson (1937, 22) have all argued for 1200–20; Meissner (1902, 42–43) proposed 1264–66, and

form the chronicle breaks off with St Óláfr's return to Norway in about 1015, and it is uncertain how much further it may originally have extended, although the prologue suggests the author intended to continue the story down to nearer his own day.[31]

These three works are manifestly interrelated; in places *Ágrip*'s text is virtually identical with that of Theodoricus, while in others it seems to agree rather with *Historia Norvegiæ*. The nature and number of correspondences between the three point to a written, rather than an oral, connection, and Siegfried Beyschlag's theory[32]—that the three synoptics independently preserve an established oral tradition—has few adherents. The scholarly literature on these works has tended to concentrate on their literary relations, and could be described, at least in comparison with the length of the works themselves, as extensive. The arguments advanced are often extraordinarily complex.[33] There is no consensus, although Theodoricus's work and *Historia Norvegiæ* are believed by most to be unconnected. It is how *Ágrip* relates to them that is anything but clear. Generally, however, *Ágrip*'s author is thought to have made direct use of Theodoricus, translating passages virtually word for word, while the similarities between *Ágrip* and *Historia Norvegiæ* are explained by most scholars as the result of their having had a common source, either Latin or Norse, although many admit that there is really nothing to preclude the possibility that *Ágrip* used *Historia Norvegiæ* directly.[34] There have been a number of candidates posited for this common source. An earlier generation of scholars assumed it to have been a Norwegian work, otherwise unattested,[35] but more recently the chief contenders have been the lost works of Sæmundr Sigfússon (1056–1133) and Ari Þorgilsson (1067/8–1148).

Maurer (1867, 226–27) a date certainly not before 1266 but possibly even as late as the fifteenth century. The dating of *Historia Norvegiæ* is obviously a key factor in any attempt to determine its position *vis-à-vis* the other Norwegian synoptics.

[31] Ulset (1983, 147–48) reckons *Historia Norvegiæ* may well have carried on until at least 1155; much the same conclusion was reached by Storm (1876, 224), but see also Schreiner 1928, 84.

[32] Beyschlag 1950, esp. 247–48.

[33] For an excellent summary of the various arguments see Andersson 1985, 201–11.

[34] See Ellehøj 1965, 198–200; Lange 1989, 164–78 and references there.

[35] See e. g. Bjarni Aðalbjarnarson 1937, 17–18, 47–49, 54.

Sæmundr, called inn fróði, 'the wise', wrote, probably in Latin, a history of the kings of Norway. This work has not survived apart from a few lines interpolated into the Icelandic translation of Oddr Snorrason's *Óláfs saga Tryggvasonar*,[36] but Sæmundr's book was also the basis for the metrical *Nóregskonungatal*, composed in Iceland at about the same time as *Ágrip* (between 1184 and 1197) and preserved in *Flateyjarbók*.[37] On the basis of the poem it is possible to get some idea of the nature and scope of Sæmundr's book, which appears to have begun with Hálfdan svarti and ended with the death of Magnús góði, although the central figures would have been Haraldr hárfagri, Hákon góði, Óláfr Tryggvason and Óláfr helgi.

Ari, also called inn fróði, is well known as the author of *Íslendingabók*, the earliest extant example of narrative prose in a Scandinavian language. References to Ari in later works indicate that his writings must have included more than the extant *Íslendingabók*, however, and indeed in the prologue to that work Ari himself states that there was an earlier version, containing *áttartala*, 'genealogy', and *konungaævi*, 'lives of kings'. What form these may have taken is not clear, but some indication is provided by Ari's own *lögsögumannaævi*, 'Lives of the Lawspeakers', in the extant *Íslendingabók*, in which the Lawspeakers are listed and the term of office given for each, along with a brief mention of the most important events during each Lawspeaker's term. This is, conceivably, the form the *konungaævi* took in the older recension of Ari's *Íslendingabók*.

In his closely-argued book *Studier over den ældste norrøne historieskrivning* Svend Ellehøj attempts to show that the common source of *Ágrip* and *Historia Norvegiæ* must have been Ari's lost *konungaævi*, and he also includes Sæmundr as one of *Ágrip*'s sources. His argument, while persuasive, is not iron-clad. But even what he, and nearly everyone else, has taken as read—that Theodoricus could not have known the works of Sæmundr and Ari because he had no written sources, and that similarities between Theodoricus and *Ágrip* can therefore only be explained as the latter having made direct use of the former—has recently been called into question. Bjarni Guðnason, reviving and augmenting an older theory,[38] has argued convincingly

---

[36] 1932, 114.

[37] II 524. On *Nóregskonungatal* see Ólafía Einarsdóttir 1964, 165–83.

[38] The idea that Theodoricus knew Ari was suggested by Árni Magnússon, see *Edda Snorra Sturlusonar* 1848–87, III 227; it has also been argued by Gjessing (1873–76, II 50–56) and Finnur Jónsson (1920–24, II 587–94).

that, despite his statements to the contrary, Theodoricus did know and use the works of Sæmundr and Ari.[39] Building on Bjarni's work, Gudrun Lange's study *Die Anfänge der isländisch-norwegischen Geschichtsschreibung* argues that not only Theodoricus but all three Norwegian synoptics *could* have used both Sæmundr and Ari, and also the original Latin version of Oddr Snorrason's *Óláfs saga Tryggvasonar* and the 'oldest saga' of Óláfr helgi. If she is right, her findings effectively put paid to the idea of a twelfth-century Norwegian school of historiography flourishing independently of the Icelandic school of Sæmundr and Ari.[40]

Ágrip's author may have had written sources other than the lost books of Sæmundr and Ari, and there has been no shortage of nominees. It has been suggested, for example, that he had access to some kind of law-book, as witnessed by his description of the 'Álfífulǫg' and their consequences in chapters XXVIII and XXIX.[41] Bjarni Aðalbjarnarson thought he must also have used a lost *Hákonar saga góða*.[42] Finnur Jónsson, among others, postulated a lost saga about the earls of Hlaðir,[43] and Didrik Arup Seip proposed Eiríkr Oddsson's lost work *Hryggjarstykki* as one of *Ágrip*'s sources.[44] These can only ever remain conjectural. As Gudrun Lange's study shows, the only thing that can be said with any certainty about *Ágrip*'s written sources is that very little indeed can be said with much certainty.

Ágrip clearly drew on oral sources as well. One such was skaldic poetry, at least some of which is likely to have come from oral tradition. The author cites seven verses: two strophes attributed to Sighvatr Þórðarson, two half-strophes—one, which he misinterprets, from the otherwise unknown poem *Oddmjór*—and three couplets which are probably to be traced to local tradition. The poet Eyvindr skáldaspillir is mentioned, along with his poem *Háleygjatal*, but no verses are cited. This is indeed unfortunate, as the verses referred to have not survived. Traces of skaldic poems have been discerned elsewhere in *Ágrip*. Bjarni Einarsson,[45] for example, detects a verse behind *Ágrip*'s description of the Icelander Þórálfr inn sterki (chapter VI)—three

---

[39] Bjarni Guðnason 1977; essentially the same theory was advanced independently in Andersson 1979.
[40] Lange 1989, 180–81.
[41] *Ágrip* 1984, xii–xiii.
[42] See e. g. Bjarni Aðalbjarnarson 1937, 54.
[43] *Ágrip* 1929, xiii.
[44] Seip 1938–39; see also Indrebø 1938–39, 61–62, and 1940.
[45] *Ágrip* 1984, xxix.

strophes from a poem about him by Þórðr Sjáreksson are cited in *Heimskringla*[46] and a further half-strophe in *Fagrskinna*.[47]

Scholars agree that one of the major sources for *Ágrip* must have been Trøndelag local tradition, which provided the Snjófríðr episode (later borrowed by Snorri) and other material of an anecdotal nature.[48]

(iii) *Style and language*

Ágrip's style is difficult to define.[49] Guðbrandur Vigfússon called it 'quaint', and for that reason 'interesting',[50] while Finnur Jónsson said: 'über den stil—wenn man überhaupt von stil sprechen kann—braucht man nicht viel zu sagen.'[51] When reading *Ágrip* one is perhaps first struck by its awkwardness. There are, to begin with, the endless compound sentences, each clause beginning with *en* ('but') or *ok* ('and'). Scattered throughout are sentences of extreme complexity—the first sentence of chapter II for example—many of which border on incomprehensibility. Some of this awkwardness, admittedly, may be due to omissions—as was mentioned above, some scholars are of the opinion that in its present form *Ágrip* is no more than a précis—or it may be that the author, working from two or more sources, has tried to cram too much into his text. Several parenthetical remarks seem particularly ill-chosen, for example the information on the size of the ship Ormr inn langi ('The Long Serpent') provided in chapter XX just as Óláfr Tryggvason is meeting his end. But given the age of the text and the fact that it is among the earliest attempts to write a continuous narrative in the vernacular to have survived, such awkwardness is perhaps not surprising.

There are, at the same time, many passages that suggest a fair degree of stylistic awareness—if not sophistication—on the part of the author. He is fond of using rhetorical figures such as antithesis: *ok bar inn sami reiði hans út, er boð hans hafði borit inn* ('the same (man) bore his anger out as had borne his message in'), *syrgði hann hana dauða, en landslýðr allr syrgði hann villtan* ('he mourned for her, dead, but the

---

[46] *Heimskringla*, I 187, 191–92.

[47] *Fagrskinna* 91–93; it is the second half of the third strophe that is not cited in *Heimskringla*.

[48] This material is most fully discussed in Indrebø 1922, 52–56.

[49] The fullest description of *Ágrip*'s style is Indrebø 1922, 20–23, from which many of the examples here derive.

[50] Guðbrandur Vigfússon 1878, lxxxvii.

[51] *Ágrip* 1929, xviii.

people all mourned for him, bewitched'), *seig hón svá í ǫsku, en konungr steig til vizku* ('she sank so into ash, but the king rose to wisdom'), or *Bjǫrn enn digri fell at hǫfði konunginum, en Þorsteinn knarrasmiðr var þegar drepinn á fœtr konunginum* ('Bjǫrn digri fell before the king, and Þorsteinn knarrasmiðr was killed right on the king's heels'). This fondness for antithesis is evident also in descriptions such as *lítil kona sýnum, en mikil rǫ́ðum* ('a woman small of stature, yet great of counsel'), or *mildr af gulli . . . en fastaldr á jǫrðum* ('open-handed with gold . . . but tight-fisted with land'), to name but two. He also repeats the same or related words, often creating neatly-balanced sentences, such as *var hennar fǫr ger prýðiliga til óprúðar* ('her journey, begun in splendour, ended in disgrace'),[52] or *ok lauk svá saurlífis-maðr í saurgu húsi sínum dǫgum ok svá ríki* ('and thus a man who had lived a life of filth ended, in a house of filth, his days and also his rule'). There are several examples of zeugma, where a single verb is used with two disparate objects, such as: *kom hann svá til trúar, því næst til Nóregs* ('he came thus to belief and then to Norway'), or *tók þá lýðr við trú, en Óláfr við ríki* ('then the people took the faith and Óláfr the kingdom'). These are doubtless to be ascribed to the author's Latin learning and are characteristic of the so-called 'courtly style', commonly found in Old Norse texts of various kinds, but particularly associated with translated romances, or *riddarasǫgur*.[53] Common, too, are alliterating collocations, particularly in personal descriptions, such as *rǫskr ok risuligr* ('valiant and imposing'), *grimmr ok greypr* ('cruel and savage'), *marglyndr ok málsnjallr, vandlyndr ok vanstilltr* ('temperamental and eloquent, irascible and intemperate'), *fastr ok fégjarn* ('mean and miserly') and so on. He also uses non-alliterating synonymous collocations, as in *í hernuð ok í víking* ('raiding and plundering'), *farin ok sløkkð* ('gone and extinguished'), *frægðar ok góðs orðlags* ('fame and good repute'), *nauð ok illing* ('evil and oppression'), *í kærleik ok í virktum* ('in favour and affection') etc. He appears also to use a kind of rhyme, for example in *grenjandi ok emjandi* ('bellowing and shrieking'), perhaps also in *fjǫlmennt ok góðmennt* ('many men and good men'). In the sentence *seig hón svá í ǫsku, en konungr steig til vizku ok hugði af heimsku*, mentioned earlier, *ǫsku—vizku—heimsku* form a kind of rhyme similar to the *skothending* commonly found in skaldic poetry. This may not, of

---

[52] See textual note c on p. 20 below.
[53] For a definition see Halvorsen 1962; several hundred examples are given in Cederschiöld 1884, v–xvi. Cf. also Jónas Kristjánsson 1981.

course, have been deliberate, but in view of the author's obvious penchant for rhetorical embellishment, it is tempting to think it was.

Ágrip preserves an unusually high number of rare words and *hapax legomena*, as well as some words not uncommon in themselves but used in an unusual way.[54] These include the adjectives *risuligr* ('tall (in stature)', normally used of buildings), *listuligr* ('magnificent'), *játsi* ('agreeing to something' + dat.), *halzi* ('in possession of something' + gen.) and *frekefldr* ('harshly-imposed'), this last occurring only in Ágrip; the nouns *vitorð* ('report' or 'knowledge', normally 'counsel'), *ím* ('doubt', normally 'dust, ashes'), *ørferð* ('fate', coupled with *ørnefni*, 'name (of a person)', normally 'place-name'),[55] *misheldi* ('ill-treatment') and *illing* ('evil'); the verb phrase *at stefja manntjón* ('to prevent loss of life'), unique to Ágrip; and the contractions *svági* (= *svá eigi*), *hérnú* (= (*sé*) *hér nú*) and *vérrum* (= *vér erum*). Also, many of the nicknames, such as *skreyja* and *heikilnefr*, are otherwise unattested and of uncertain meaning. Unusual grammatical forms include *hvak*, strong preterite of the verb *hvika* ('to waver'), normally *hvikaði*;[56] *sløri*, also spelt *sleri*, preterite of the verb *slá* ('to strike'), normally *sló*;[57] *segr*, third person singular of *segja* ('to say'), normally *segir*; *viðrtalan* ('conversation'), normally *við(r)tal*; *stí* ('sty'), n., normally *stía*, f.; and *djákn* ('deacon'), n., normally *djákn(i)*, m.

The text contains only a few loan words, for example the Latin word *propheta*; *kempa* ('champion'), instead of the older *kappi*; *fróva*, from Low German; and *kurteiss*, one of the very first words borrowed into Old Norse from French.

Editorial principles

(i) *Orthography and morphology*

The orthography of the manuscript, as was mentioned above, is somewhat idiosyncratic and more than usually inconsistent, particularly as regards the representation of vowels in accented syllables.[58] For the purposes of the present edition it was thought best to normalise the

---

[54] I am grateful to Christopher Sanders of Den arnamagnæanske kommissions ordbog for his assistance in checking these words and forms.
[55] See Johannisson 1939, 99–101.
[56] The form *hvak* is otherwise unattested; see Noreen 1923, § 498, Anm. 8.
[57] See Noreen 1923, § 501, Anm. 2; § 506.
[58] See Ágrip 1880, vi–xvii.

orthography of the text along the lines used in the series *Íslenzk fornrit*. This has meant, for example, that although the voiced and unvoiced dental spirants /ð/ and /þ/ are both normally written *þ* in the manuscript, in keeping with early Icelandic (but not Norwegian) scribal practice,[59] the present edition normalises. Similarly, there is no apparent pattern in the distribution of the characters *u*, *v* and *y* in the manuscript,[60] but their use has been fully normalised here, as has the representation of intervocalic /f/ and the use of *i* and *j*, of which the last occurs only sporadically in the manuscript as an orthographic variant of /i/.[61] Both *c* and *ch* occur frequently in the manuscript for /k/, and /kk/ is normally written *ck*, while /kv/ is written *qu*;[62] in all these cases the present edition normalises. Normalised too has been the use of *z*, which in the manuscript is used (as it was in Icelandic orthography until well into the sixteenth century[63]) for a dental + /s/, for example in gen. sg. forms such as *malz* (= 'malts'), *lanz* (= 'lands'), or *halvarz* (= 'Hallvarðs'), and is also used after /ll/ or /nn/, e. g. *alz* (= 'alls'), *mannz* (= 'manns'). In the present edition, however, *z* is used as it was in official Icelandic orthography up until 1973, i. e. in the second person plural and past participles of middle voice verbs and in words where a dental has been assimilated to /s/, e. g. *íslenzka*.[64] Finally, geminate consonants are almost invariably written as single when followed by another consonant—normal practice in Icelandic until the nineteenth century[65]—e. g. in 'allt', written *alt*, or 'sløkkð', written *slaucþ*; these are fully normalised, as are the many instances of geminate consonants written as single and vice versa.[66]

In unaccented syllables *i* is much commoner than *e*, occurring nearly seven times as often. Conversely, *o* occurs more frequently than *u*, in

---

[59] Hreinn Benediktsson 1965, 21–22. There are a few sporadic examples of *ð* in the manuscript, but for /d/ rather than /ð/.

[60] See Hreinn Benediktsson 1965, 25–26.

[61] This is entirely typical for Icelandic manuscripts generally, see Hreinn Benediktsson 1965, 46.

[62] See Hreinn Benediktsson 1965, 30–34.

[63] See e. g. Noreen 1923, §§ 43, 238.2 d, 245.1; Alexander Jóhannesson 1923–24, § 273; and Bandle 1956, §§ 108.2, 114.

[64] On the (rather unusual) use of *þ* for /z/ in the manuscript, e. g. *beþt* for 'bezt', see Brieskorn 1909, 160–66.

[65] See Jón Aðalsteinn Jónsson 1959, esp. 86, 90, 96; this practice is followed by Finnur Jónsson is his edition (*Ágrip* 1929).

[66] See *Ágrip* 1880, xvii; some of these (e. g. *settia* for 'setja', *fittiom* for 'Fitjum') may derive from the Norwegian exemplar; see Seip 1955, 113.

a proportion of roughly three to one.[67] These have been fully normalised, so that *i* and *u* are used throughout.

Vowels in accented syllables have been normalised in accordance with accepted editorial practice, with the exception that in the present edition the clear distinction made in the manuscript between /á/ and its *u*-mutated form /ǫ́/ is preserved.[68] These two phonemes had fallen together in Icelandic by 1250,[69] or well before the date of the vast majority of extant vernacular manuscripts, so that this distinction is not usually made in normalised editions, other than in verses attributed to skalds from the twelfth century and earlier.

The following exceptions to common practice have also been made:

1. The proper name 'Magnús' is normally written *ma‹gnus*, i. e. with mutated vowel; I have spelt this form of the name *Mǫgnús*. The few instances of unmutated /a/ have been allowed to stand.

2. 'Norwegianisms', i. e. instances of unmutated /a/,[70] and where /h/ is lacking before /r/ and /l/,[71] have been allowed to stand, e. g. *kallað*, *reyr*, *lut*.

3. Superlative forms of 'góðr' are frequently written with *a*, e. g. *baztir*; these have been allowed to stand.

4. Forms of the word 'sonr' (other than dat. sg. and nom. pl.) occur most frequently with *u* when written in full; where abbreviated, expansion has been in keeping with this practice. When they occur, however, forms with *o* have been preserved.

5. The combination /pt/, as in 'eptir' and 'aptr',[72] is consistently written *ft*, at least by the principal hand, and the present edition therefore prints *eftir*, *aftr* etc.

In addition to these, individual spellings felt to be of interest (i. e. those with a basis in phonology, rather than in scribal caprice) have been allowed to stand, or are mentioned in a note. There is as a result a certain degree of inconsistency in the orthography of the edition.

[67] This is, again, quite in keeping with other manuscripts of the period; see Hreinn Benediktsson 1962.

[68] The latter is represented in the manuscript by the characters *a̔*, *o* and *ǫ*; rarely by *a* except in Hand II.

[69] See Noreen 1923, § 107; when nasalised, /ǫ́/ had fallen together with /ó/ by the mid-eleventh century, see Noreen 1923, § 116; Hreinn Benediktsson 1965, 61–62.

[70] See Seip 1955, 123–27.

[71] See Seip 1955, 48; there are no instances of lack of /h/ before /n/.

[72] See Noreen 1923, § 240.2.

Variant spellings such as *friðla* and *frilla*, *gersimi* and *gǫrsimi*, have been allowed to stand, as have the various forms of the definite article, which appear written both with *i* and *e*.

In general, 'aberrant' morphological forms have been retained. There is, for example, a good deal of variation in forms of the indefinite pronoun 'nǫkkurr'. In each case the form found in the manuscript has been used, although the spelling has been normalised. The variant forms 'fyr' for 'fyrir' and 'miðal' for 'meðal' and older forms such as 'vas' and 'umb' are preserved when they occur. Similarly, 'þessur', nom. and acc. n. pl. of the demonstrative pronoun 'sjá', another 'Norwegianism',[73] occurs four times and is retained.

Obvious or probable errors have been corrected; missing letters (i. e. those mistakenly omitted rather than assimilated) are supplied in angle brackets; misspellings are corrected in the text and the original reading given in a footnote.

Words or letters which cannot now be read are supplied in square brackets; where these have been erased and cannot be reconstructed the present edition prints [ooo], the number of os indicating the probable number of letters missing.

(ii) *Punctuation, chapter division etc.*

The only mark of punctuation used in the manuscript is the point, but even this is used neither consistently nor in keeping with modern practice. The punctuation and capitalisation in the present edition are therefore entirely editorial. The practice of the manuscript has, however, been allowed to influence the placing of stops and other marks of punctuation to some extent—in not, for example, preceding *er* by a comma in restrictive (defining) relative clauses as is normally done in, for example, *Íslenzk fornrit*.

I have chosen to separate with commas, rather than stops, the large numbers of 'subjectless' sentences beginning with *en* or *ok*. In places I have resorted to using dashes to enclose a parenthetical remark.

The text is quite clearly divided into chapters. These are unnumbered in the manuscript and without headings. Some of the chapters, it will be noted, are extremely short, e. g. chapter XXX,[74] and several

[73] See Noreen 1923, § 470; Seip 1955, 197.

[74] Although this is marked in the manuscript as a separate chapter, Bjarni Einarsson (*Ágrip* 1984, 29) incorporates it into the previous chapter, where it logically belongs. I have chosen to follow the manuscript, as did Finnur Jónsson in his edition (*Ágrip* 1929, 31). After chapter XXIX, therefore, my chapter numbers are one higher than those of the *ÍF* edition.

begin in awkward places, chapter L being perhaps the most obvious case. Nearly three-quarters of the chapters begin with the word *En*. In the edition this division, however awkward, is retained. Chapter numbers are obviously editorial and do not take into account any chapter divisions that may have occurred in the lacunae.

There are no paragraph divisions in the manuscript, although when a sentence happens to begin a new line it will occasionally begin with a slightly larger capital drawn in the margin. I have chosen to ignore these. In the manuscript the verses are written as prose and their arrangement here is therefore also editorial.

Numbers in the text are most often written with roman numerals, normally preceded and followed by points. I have chosen to retain this form of notation in the present edition, normalising to the extent that I have sets points before and after whether they appear in the manuscript or not.

(iii) *Previous editions and translations*

Ágrip has been edited and translated several times, although never before into English in its entirety.[75] In 1834 P. A. Munch published an edition together with a Danish translation under the title 'Brudstykke af en gammel norsk Kongesaga' in *Samlinger til det norske Folks Sprog og Historie* II, 273–335. The following year an edition by Finnur Magnússon, 'Stutt ágrip af Noregs konúnga sögum', appeared in the tenth volume of the series *Fornmanna sögur* (1835), 377–421. This edition was the basis for a Danish translation by N. M. Petersen, 'Kort Omrids af de norske Kongers Sagaer', published in *Oldnordiske Sagaer* X (1836), 329–71, and a Latin translation by Sveinbjörn Egilsson, 'Epitome historiarum regum Norvegicorum', in *Scripta historica Islandorum* X (1841), 350–92. In 1880 Verner Dahlerup produced a diplomatic edition, *Ágrip af Noregs konunga sögum: Diplomatarisk udgave*, in the series published by *Samfundet til udgivelse af gammel nordisk litteratur* (1880)—probably the most 'diplomatic' edition ever produced in Old Norse–Icelandic studies[76]—which incorporated many readings from an unpublished transcription of the text made by Gustav Storm (see *Ágrip* 1880, xxxvii; several of these are referred to in the

---

[75] Margaret Ashdown 1930, 144–51 (textual notes pp. 208–16), includes a normalised text with facing English translation of the section of *Ágrip* from chapter XVI to the beginning of chapter XXIII in the present edition.

[76] Two columns of text were printed, equally 'diplomatically', in Konráð Gíslason 1846, xxxix–xl.

textual notes below). Finnur Jónsson edited *Ágrip* for *Altnordische Saga-Bibliothek* XVIII (1929). Several years later Gustav Indrebø produced a normalised edition with facing Norwegian translation, *Ågrip: Ei liti norsk kongesoge*, in *Norrøne bokverk* XXXII (1936; revised edition 1973). Finally, there is Bjarni Einarsson's edition, *Ágrip af Nóregskonunga sǫgum*, in *Íslenzk fornrit* XXIX (1984).

A note on the translation

In my translation of the text I have endeavoured to reproduce as closely as possible the Old Norse original, producing, I hope, a result which is, if not always fair, at least true. The conventions of English grammar and syntax have, however, often necessitated the rearrangement of clauses within a sentence and not infrequently the addition of grammatical subjects.

I have not translated the Old Norse nicknames, partially as a result of my own dissatisfaction with renderings such as 'paunch-shaker' for *þambarskelmir* or 'shock-head' for *lúfa*, but also because of my feeling that a man's name—and Norse nicknames were names—is his name, however accessible its meaning may be. Translations are provided in the notes or in the index. I have also refrained from anglicising personal and place-names, although I have 'translated' names of countries where they correspond to modern political entities like Norway, Sweden and Denmark, and have given Anglo-Saxon names, Æthelstan for example, their accepted English form. Most of the personal names in *Ágrip* have no counterpart in English, however, and while names such as 'Ragenwald' may have set the hearts of nineteenth-century Englishmen a-racing, I felt nothing would be gained by the use of forms foreign to both English-speakers and Scandinavians. Where English equivalents do exist—Eric, Swen, Harold, Canute—I have for the sake of consistency not used them. I have retained for the most part the Old Norse forms of place-names, even in cases where there is a clear modern Scandinavian counterpart, in the belief that Niðaróss, for example, is a very different place from Trondheim. I give the modern-day equivalents in the notes and index and maps are provided for any readers who might wish to undertake a pilgrimage to the saga-steads of Scandinavia.

Ágrip af Nóregskonungasǫgum

A synoptic history of the kings of Norway

Ágrip af Nóregskonungasǫgum

I. [... var] hann þá einn tekinn til [konungs]. Var hann þá kallaðr [Haral]dr lúfa, þvíat maðrinn var þá eigi [hárfa]gr, en síðan b[rey]ttisk nafn hans ok var kallaðr Haraldr h[ár]fagri, þvíat manna va[r hann] listuligastr ok hærðr bezt. En hér hœfir at skýra spurdaga[a] þann er kristnir menn gera, hvat heiðnir menn myndu til jóla vita, með því at jól vǫr eru risin af burð dróttins várs. Heiðnir menn gerðu sér samkundu ok í tígn við Óðin, en Óðinn heitir mǫrgum nǫfnum. Hann heitir Viðrir ok hann heitir Hǫr ok Þriði ok Jólni⟨r⟩, ok var af Jólni jól kalluð. En sjá er hǫttr á dauðdaga Hálfdanar: hann þá veizlu á Haðalandi, en þá er hann fór þaðan í sleða, [þá drukkna]ði hann í Rǫnd [í R]ykinvík, þar er nautabrunnr var, ok var fœrðr til Steins síðan á Hringaríki ok var þar heygðr.

II. Haraldr tók eftir Hálfdan ríki þat er faðir hans hafði haft, ok aflaði sér meira ríkis með þeim hætti—er maðrinn var snemma rǫskr ok risuligr vexti—at hann helt orrostu við næsta konunga ok sigraði alla, ok eignaðisk hann fyrstr konunga einn Nóreg á tvítøgs[b] aldri, ok helt ena síðurstu orrostu við konung þann er Skeiðar-Brandr hét, í Hafrsvági fyr Jaðri, ok flýði Brandr til Danmarkar ok fell í orrostu á Vinnlandi, sem segir í kvæði því er heitir Oddmjór, er gǫrt er umb konungatal, með þessum orðum:

    1. Skjǫldungr rak með skildi
       Skeiðar-Brand ór landi;
       réð sá konungr síðan
       snjallr Nóregi ǫllum.

---

[a] written spurdadaga (over line division).
[b] following this word there is an empty space, about one third of the line (1.5 cm).

A synoptic history of the kings of Norway

I. . . . he was then taken as sole king. He was then called Haraldr lúfa,[1] for he was not then fine-haired, but later his name changed and he was called Haraldr hárfagri, because he was the handsomest of men and finest-haired.

Here it is fitting to elucidate a problem posed by Christian men as to what heathen men knew about Yule, for our Yule has its origin in the birth of Our Lord. Heathen men had a feast, held in honour of Óðinn, and Óðinn is called by many names: he is called Viðrir and he is called Hár and Þriði and Jólnir; and it is after Jólnir that Yule is named.[2]

This is how Hálfdan[3] died: he was being feasted[4] in Haðaland, and leaving there in a sledge he drowned in Rǫnd in Rykinvík, where there was a hole in the ice for cattle; and he was taken to Steinn in Hringaríki and there buried in a mound.[5]

II. Haraldr succeeded Hálfdan in the kingdom his father had had and enlarged his kingdom—he was valiant at an early age and of imposing stature—by fighting battles with neighbouring kings and defeating them all, and by the age of twenty he was the first king to gain all Norway. He fought his final battle with a king named Skeiðar-Brandr, in Hafrsvágr,[6] off Jaðarr. Brandr fled to Denmark and fell in a battle in Wendland, as is told in the poem Oddmjór,[7] which was composed about the kings of Norway, in this way:

> 1. The Scylding-king[8] drove with shield
> Skeiðar-Brandr[9] from land;
> the king thereafter governed,
> valiant, Norway all.

Ágrip af Nóregskonungasǫgum

En þat var .x. vetr er hann barðisk áðr til lands en hann yrði allvaldskonungr at Nóregi, ok siðaði vel land sitt ok friðaði, ok átti sunu tvítján ok með mǫrgum konum, kómu þó tveir einir til konungs nafns, Eiríkr blóðax ok Hǫkon góði. Var Eiríkr blóðax ⟨í⟩ elzta lagi sona hans, annarr Hǫkon í yngsta lagi, er Aðalsteinn Englands konungr tók í sunar stað, þriði Óláfr digrbeinn, .iiij. Bjǫrn kaupmaðr, ⟨er⟩ sumir kalla bunu, .v. Goðormr, .vj. Hálfdan svarti, .vij. Dagr, .viij. Hringr, .ix. Goðrøðr skirja, .x. Rǫgnvaldr, .xi. Sigtryggr, .xij. Fróði, .xiij. Hrœrekr, .xiiij. Tryggvi, .xv. Gunnrøðr, .xvj. Eysteinn, .xvij. Sigurðr hrísi, .xviij. Guðrøðr ljómi, .xix. Há⟨l⟩fdan[a] hvítbeinn, er sumir kǫlluðu háfœtu, .xx. Rǫgnvaldr reykill, er sumir kalla Ragnar, er var sunr Finnkonu einnar er kǫlluð var Snjófríð,[b] dóttir Svása Finnkonungs, ok brá hónum til móður sinnar. Var hann kallaðr seiðmaðr—þat er spámaðr—ok var staðfastr á Haðalandi ok síddi þar ok var kallaðr skratti.

III. Jólaaftan, er Haraldr sat at mat, þá kom Svási fyrir dyrr ok sendi konungi boð at hann skyldi út ganga til hans, en[c] konungr bráusk reiðr við þeim sendiboðum, ok bar inn sami reiði hans út er boð hans hafði borit inn. En hinn[d] bað hann þá eigi fyrir því at síðr [í] annat sinni ok gaf hónum bjórskinn eitt til, ok kvað sik vera þann Finninn er hann hafði ját at setja gamma sinn annan veg brekkunnar á Þoptyn, þar sem þá var konungrinn. En konungrinn gekk út ok varð hónum þess játsi, at hann gekk yfir í gamma hans með áeggjan[e] sumra sinna manna, þóat sumir letti. Stóð þar upp Snjófríð, dóttir Svása, kvenna vænust, ok byrlaði ker mjaðar fullt konunginum, ok hann tók allt

---

[a] *the lack of* l *may be a Norwegian dialectal feature*; cf. Noreen 1923, § 297 and Anm. 1; Seip 1955, 76, 109–10, 164.
[b] *here and below the nom. ending* r *is lacking*, cf. Noreen 1923, § 384, Anm. 2.
[c] MS er.
[d] MS ħ (*i. e.* hann), *but corrected below line.*
[e] *written* aengiaɴ; *cf.* engiar (= Eggjar) *below, note a on p.* 42.

It was ten winters he fought for the country, before becoming sole ruler of Norway, and he brought good order and peace to his country. Haraldr had twenty sons, and by many women,[10] though only two came to be kings, Eiríkr blóðøx and Hákon góði. Eiríkr blóðøx was the eldest of his sons and Hákon the youngest, whom Æthelstan, king of England, fostered; third was Óláfr digrbeinn; fourth Bjǫrn kaupmaðr, whom some call buna; fifth Goðormr; sixth Hálfdan svarti; seventh Dagr; eighth Hringr; ninth Guðrøðr skirja; tenth Rǫgnvaldr; eleventh Sigtryggr; twelfth Fróði; thirteenth Hrœrekr; fourteenth Tryggvi; fifteenth Gunnrøðr; sixteenth Eysteinn; seventeenth Sigurðr hrísi; eighteenth Guðrøðr ljómi; nineteenth Hálfdan hvítbeinn, whom some called háfœta; and the twentieth Rǫgnvaldr reykill, whom some call Ragnarr. He was the son of a certain Lappish woman called Snjófríðr,[11] the daughter of Svási, king of the Lapps, and took after his mother. He was called a sorcerer—that is to say a soothsayer—and he lived in Haðaland and practised sorcery there and was called a warlock.[12]

III. On the eve of Yule,[13] as Haraldr sat at table, Svási came to the door and sent word in to the king that he should come out to him. This request angered the king, and the same man bore his anger out as had borne the message in. Svási asked him nevertheless a second time and also gave him a beaver skin and said that he was that Lapp whom the king had allowed to set up his hut on the other side of the hill at Þoptyn, where the king then was. The king went out and he agreed to go to Svási's hut, egged on by some of his men, though others tried to dissuade him.

There Snjófríðr stood up, Svási's daughter, the most beautiful of women and offered the king a cup full of mead. He took it and with it her hand, and suddenly it was

saman ok hǫnd hennar. Ok þegar var[a] sem eldshiti kœmi í hǫrund hans ok vildi þegar hafa hana á þeiri nótt. En Svási sagði at þat mundi eigi vera, nema hónum nauðgum,[b] nema konungrinn festi hana ok fengi at lǫgum. Ok hann festi ok fekk ok unni svá með œrslum, at ríki sitt ok allt þat er hans tígn byrjaði þá fyrlét hann ok sat hjá henni nótt ok dag náliga,[c] meðan þau lifðu bæði, ok .iij. vetr síðan hón var dauð. Syrgði hann hana dauða, en landslýðr allr syrgði hann villtan.

IV. En þessa villu at lægja kom[d] til læknanar Þorleif⟨r⟩ spaki, er með viti lægði[e] þá villu ok með eftirmæli með þessum hætti: 'Eigi er, konungr, kynligt, attu[f] munir svá fríða konu ok kynstóra, ok tígnir hana á dúni ok á guðvefi sem hón bað þik. En tígn þín er þó minni en hœfir—ok hennar—í því at hón liggr of lengi í sama fatnaði. Er myklu sannligra at hón sé hrœrð.' Ok þegar er hón var hrœrð, þá sløri á óþefjani ok ýldu ok hverskyns illum fnyk af líkamanum. Var þá hvatat báli ok hón brennd. Blánaði þó áðr allr líkaminn, ok ullu ór ormar ok eðlur, froskar ok pǫddur, ok allskyns illyrmi. Seig hón svá í ǫsku, en konungr steig til vizku ok hugði af heimsku, stýrði síðan ríki sínu ok styrkði; gladdisk hann af þegnum sínum, ok þegnar af hónum, en ríkit af hvǫru tveggja, ok sat at Nóregi einvaldskonungr sex tøgu vetra síðan, er hann hafði innan tíu vetra aflat alls Nóregs, andaðisk síðan á Rogalandi ok var heygðr á Haugum upp frá Hasleyjarsundi.

V. En eftir Harald tók Eiríkr blóðøx[g] við ríki, en Hǫkon bróðir hans var vestr í Englandi með Aðalsteini konungi,

---
[a] MS com.
[b] hónum nauðgum] the word at may be lacking here.
[c] added above the line.
[d] MS coma (over line division).
[e] lægði] thus Heimskringla I 126; MS lagþe.
[f] attu] i. e. at þú; tu added above the line.
[g] here written blǫt a/x, but elsewhere with þ.

as if fiery heat entered into his flesh and he wished to have her that same night. But Svási said that this should not be so—except against his will—unless the king betrothed himself to her and then wedded her according to the law. And he betrothed himself to her and wedded her and loved her so witlessly that he neglected his kingdom and all that beseemed his kingly honour, and he stayed by her almost night and day while they both lived and for three years after she died. He mourned for her, dead, but the people all mourned for him, bewitched.

IV. But Þorleifr spaki came to cure him and put an end to this enchantment, and he did it wisely and with blandishments in this way: 'It is not strange, king, that you should remember so beautiful and noble a woman and honour her thus on down and velvet, as she asked you. And yet your honour is less than is fitting—and hers—for she has lain too long in the same clothes. It would be much seemlier if she were moved.' And when she was moved there issued from the body a rank and fulsome stench and foul odours of every sort. A pyre was hastily prepared and she was burnt, but before that the body blackened and there bubbled out worms and vipers, frogs and toads and multitudes of vermin. She sank thus into ash, but the king rose to wisdom and abandoned his folly; he from then on took control of his kingdom and strengthened it; he was gladdened by his subjects and they by him and the kingdom by them both, and he ruled Norway as absolute king for sixty years thereafter, after having won all of it in ten. He later died in Rogaland and was buried at Haugar, inland from Hasleyjarsund.[14]

V. Eiríkr blóðøx took the kingdom after Haraldr. His brother Hákon was west in England with King Æthelstan, to whom

er faðir hans lífs hafði hann sendan til fóstrs. Eiríkr blóðax var fríðr sýnum, mikill ok inn virðiligsti. Hann átti Gunnhildi, dóttur Ǫzurar lafskeggs—þeira synir vǫru þeir Gamli ok Goðormr, Haraldr gráfeldr ok Erling⟨r⟩, Sigurðr slefa; enn eru nefndir fleiri, Goðrøðr ljómi ok Ragnfrøðr, Hálfdan ok Eyvindr ok Gormr—ok helt Nóregi .v. vetr alls með þeim tveim vetrum er hónum var fyr konung heilsat í landinu þá er Haraldr lifði, en þrjá síðan. Gunnhildr kona hans var allra kvenna fegrst, lítil kona sýnum en mikil rǫ́ðum. Hón gørðisk svá illrǫ́ðug, en hann svá áhlýðinn til grimmleiks ok til allskyns áþjánar við lýðinn, at þungt var at bera. Hann réð[a] Óláf digrbein, bróður sinn, ok Bjǫrn ok fleiri brœðr sína. Því var hann kallaðr blóðøx at maðrinn var [ooooo] ofstopamaðr ok greypr, ok allra mest af rǫ́ðum hennar. Þá kvǫddu vitrir menn Hǫ́kon aftr í land með leynd tveim vetrum eftir andlát Haralds hárfagra, ok hann kømr tveim skipum vestan ok sat svá um vetr at hann hafði eigi konungs nafn.[b] Hǫ́kon var manna vænstr, mikill ok listuligr, ok svá sterkr [oooo][c] at engvir fengusk hónum jafnir. Hann var hǫfði ǫllu hæri en aðrir menn, hárit þat á hǫfði sem silki gult væri. Hann var [í][d] ǫllum ridderaskap ok korteisi um fram of aðra menn. Hann var náliga tvítøgr er hann kom í land. En hónum tók brátt svá flokkr at vaxa at Eiríkr mátti þá eigi viðstǫðu hafa, ok flýði hann þá ok kona hans til Danmarkar fyrst. En Hǫ́kon sat þá einn konungr at Nóregi, ok var Nóregr svá góðr undir hans ríki at hann var eigi munaðr betri, fyr útan þat at eigi var kristni á. En hann var kristinn ok átti konu heiðna ok veik mjǫk af kristninni fyr hennar sakar ok fyr vildar sakar við lýðinn er á mót stóð kristninni, helt þó sunnudags helgi ok frjádaga

[a] *more commonly* réð af dǫgum.
[b] nafn] *written* nāfn (= nanfn *or* namfn), *cf. note a on p. 48.*
[c] *there is a short erasure at the end of the line followed by another, even shorter, at the beginning of the next line; as the text appears, here as elsewhere, to have been unaffected, one could imagine an original* uar h̄ (= var hann).
[d] *this word appears to have been erased.*

his father, while alive, had sent him to be fostered. Eiríkr blóðøx was a handsome man, tall and very stately. His wife was Gunnhildr, daughter of Ǫzurr lafskegg.[15] Their sons were Gamli and Goðormr, Haraldr gráfeldr and Erlingr, Sigurðr slefa; there are still more named: Guðrøðr ljómi, Ragnfrøðr, Hálfdan, Eyvindr and Gormr. Eiríkr ruled Norway for five years, including the two years he was considered king while Haraldr lived and three years thereafter.[16]

Gunnhildr, his wife, was of all women the most beautiful; a woman small of stature yet great of counsel. She became so wicked in her counsel, and he so easily led to acts cruel and oppressive to the people, that it was hard to bear. He had killed his brother Óláfr digrbeinn and Bjǫrn and others of his brothers. Thus he was called blóðøx, because he was a cruel and ruthless man, and mostly as a result of her counsel.[17]

Then, two years after the death of Haraldr hárfagri, wise men, in secrecy, called Hákon back to Norway. He came from the west with two ships and stayed there the winter without the name of king. Hákon was the best-looking of men, tall and magnificent, and so strong that his equal could not be found. He was a full head taller than other men and his hair was like yellow silk. In chivalry and all courtesy he excelled other men. He was nearly twenty when he came to the country.

His following grew so quickly that Eiríkr could not stand against him, and he and his wife fled, going first to Denmark.[18] Hákon ruled thereafter alone as king of Norway, and Norway so prospered under his rule that none could remember when it had been better—except that there was then no Christianity. Hákon was a Christian, but his wife was heathen,[19] and he departed much from Christian ways for her sake and in order to please the people, who stood against Christianity, although he kept the holiness of Sunday and the Friday fast.

fǫstu. Hǫkon fór til Danmarkar suðr tveim skipum ok barðisk þar ok hrauð .x. skip með tveim skipum. Í þeiri fǫr lagði hann undir sik Selund[a] ok Skáney ok Gautland et vestra, ok helt svá aftr í Nóreg. Á hans dǫgum snørusk margir menn til kristni af vinsældum hans, en sumir hǫfnuðu blótum, þótt eigi kristnaðisk.[b] Hann reisti nekkverar kirkjur í Nóregi ok setti lærða menn at, en þeir brenndu kirkjurnar ok vǫgu prestana fyrir hónum, svát hann mátti eigi því halda fyr illvirkjum þeira. Ok þar eftir gerðu Þrœndir fǫr at hónum á Mærini ok bǫ́ðu hann blóta sem aðra konunga í Nóregi, 'ella rekum vér þik af ríki, nema þú gerir nekkvern hlut í samþykki eftir oss'. En fyr því at hann sá ákafa þeira [ooooooooooooooo] á hǫnd hónum [oooooo][c] at hǫfðingja ráði, þá snøri hann svá til, at hann fyrkvað eigi í nekkverum hlut í yfirbragði til vingunar við þá. Svá er sagt at hann biti á hrosslifr, ok svá at hann brá dúki umb, ok beit eigi bera, en blótaði eigi ǫðruvís, en svá er sagt at síðan gekk hónum allt þyngra en áðr. Hann setti Golaþingslǫg eftir ráðagørð Þorleifs spaka, er verit hafði forðum. En þá er hann hafði .xv. vetr haldit Nóregi með vinsæld ok með friði, þá sóttu synir Eiríks blóðøxar í Nóreg[d]—Gamli Gunnhildarsunr, er þeira brœðra var œztr ok vaskligastr at gervǫllu, ok Goðormr ok Haraldr gráfeldr ok allir þeir brœðr—ok heldu [oooooo][e] orrostu í Kǫrmt við Ǫgvaldsnes við Hókon [oooooooooooooooo][f]—þar fell Goðormr, Hálfdan, Eyvindr, en aðrir kómusk á flótta undan—en aðra orrostu litlu síðarr í Fræði enn við Hókon, ok varð Hókon enn øfri, en þeir brœðr flýðu ór landi allir nema Gamli. Hann flýði til lands

---

[a] *written* Selundr, *but* r *erased.*

[b] t *added above the line; there are three other examples of* crisn-, *however, cf. notes* b *on p.* 30, a *on p.* 34 *and* b *on p.* 74.

[c] *here the first letter could conceivably be* s *and the last* i; *Storm reconstructed* snæri (*see* Ágrip *1880, 102*).

[d] *MS* noregi, *i. e. dat. instead of acc.*

[e] *here a word of about six letters has been erased, conceivably* fyrsta.

[f] *here nearly an entire line has been erased.*

Hákon went south to Denmark with two ships and fought there, defeating ten ships with his two. On this voyage he won Sjóland, Skáney and Vestra-Gautland and then returned to Norway.

In his day many men turned to Christianity as a result of his popularity, and others, although they did not become Christian, ceased the practice of pagan rites. He built some churches in Norway and set clerics in them, but the heathens burnt his churches and killed his priests so that he could not continue this activity as a result of their evil work. And later the Prœndir[20] rose against him at Mærin and asked him to worship the gods as other kings in Norway had done. 'We will drive you from the kingdom,' they said, 'if you do not act in some way in accordance with our wishes.' Because he saw their zeal against him, and following the advice of the chieftains, he responded in such a way that he refused nothing, so as to appear to appease them.

It is said that he bit horse-liver, but wrapped it in cloth so that he should not bite it directly. He would worship in no other way, and thereafter, it is said, his troubles were greater than before.[21]

He established the Gulaþing Law, following the advice of Þorleifr spaki, as it had been of old.[22]

After he had ruled Norway for fifteen years with peace and popularity, the sons of Eiríkr blóðøx returned to Norway: Gamli Gunnhildarson,[23] who of the brothers was foremost and most valiant in every way, and Goðormr and Haraldr gráfeldr and all the brothers. They fought Hákon in battle in Kǫrmt, near Ǫgvaldsnes. There fell Goðormr and Hálfdan and Eyvindr, but the others fled and escaped. Another battle was fought shortly thereafter against Hákon in Fræði,[24] and again Hákon won. The brothers all fled the country, with the exception of Gamli, who went to the

ok it[a] øfra of Súrnadal til Þróndheims, en menn Hǫkonar með lýðsins[b] fulltingi[c] sóttu á mót hónum ok felldu í Gaulardali, þar sem nú er kallat Gamlaleir af hans nafni.

VI. En því næst á .ix. vetra fresti síz þeir brœðr hafðu í Nóreg sótt með bardaga, þá heldu þeir brœðr er eftir vǫru —Haraldr gráfeldr, er þeira var merkilegastr at Gamla fallinn—með Gunnhildi móður sinni aftr í land, ok heldu orrostu við Hǫkon á Fitjum í Storð hjá Byskupssteini. Þar vǫru fjórir of einn á mót Hǫkoni. Þar var með þeim í því liði sá maðr er hét Eyvindr skreyja.[d] Hann var kappi mikill, meiri en aðrir menn, ok bitu varla jǫrn. Hann gekk svá umb daginn at ekki vétta helt við hónum, þvíat engi hafði fǫng á í móti hónum. Hann fór svá grenjandi ok emjandi, ok ruddi svá at hann hjó á báðar hendr ok spurði hvar hann Norðmanna konungr væri, 'hví leynisk hann nú?' 'Haltu svá vel[e] fram ef þú vill hann hitta,' kvað konungrinn, en hann œstisk at meir við, ok hjó á báðar hendr með mikilli breiðri øxi svá at[f] í jǫrðu nam staðar. Þá mælti Þórálfr enn sterki, íslenzkr maðr, er þá var með konunginum, nítján vetra gamall ok kallaðr var jamsterkr konunginum: 'Villtu, herra,' kvað hann, 'at ek róðumsk í mót hónum?' 'Nei,' kvað hann, 'mik vill hann hitta; skal hann ok því mik finna,' varp af hǫfði sér dulhetti er ⟨Eyvindr⟩ skáldaspillir hafði sett á hjálm [oo][g] gollroðinn er konungrinn hafði á hǫfði til leyndar, at þá væri hann torkenndri [oooo] en áðr, þvíat hann var auðkenndr fyr hæðar sakar ok yfirbragðs. Síðan gekk konungrinn undan merkjunum fram í mót hónum kappanum, í silkiskyrtu ok hjálm á hǫfði, skjǫld fyr sér, en sverð í hendi er Kvernbiti hét, ok sýndisk maðrinn svá

---

[a] MS in.
[b] s added above the line, incorrectly, before ð.
[c] MS fvltilgi.
[d] written scraygia.
[e] added above the line.
[f] first written svat (cf. p. 14), but with a second a added above the line.
[g] possibly not an erasure.

mainland and then overland through Súrnadalr to Þrándheimr. Hákon's men, with the help of the people, came against him and killed him in Gaulardalr, at that place which is now called Gamlaleir after him.[25]

VI. But then, nine years[26] after the brothers attacked Norway, Haraldr gráfeldr—who was the most noteworthy of the brothers after the death of Gamli—and those brothers who remained came back to the country with their mother Gunnhildr and fought a battle with Hákon at Fitjar in Storð, near Byskupssteinn. They were four to one against Hákon.

In their army was a man named Eyvindr skreyja.[27] He was a great champion, bigger than other men, and little iron could bite him. He fought that day in such a way that none could stand against him, for no one could have power against him. He went bellowing and shrieking forward, clearing a path by hacking on both sides, demanding where the Norwegian king was; 'Why does he hide now?'

'Keep on as you are, if you would find him,' said the king, and at this Eyvindr grew more violent and hewed on both sides with a great broad axe, striking down to the ground each time. Þórálfr sterki,[28] an Icelander who was then with the king, nineteen years old and said to be as strong as the king himself, spoke then: 'Do you wish, my lord,' he said, 'that I attack him?'

'No,' said the king, 'it is I he wishes to meet; so meet me he shall.' And he threw off the hood Eyvindr skáldaspillir[29] had placed over the golden helmet he had on his head, in order to hide him so that he would be more difficult to recognise—for his height and bearing made him easily known. Then the king went out from under his banner and faced the warrior, wearing a silk shirt, a helmet on his head, a shield before him, and in his hand the sword called Kvernbiti,[30] and thus dressed he seemed to all falcon-like.

búinn ǫllum [ooooo]ᵃ haukligr. Þá óð kappinn at fram hjálmaðr ok brynjaðrᵇ í mót ok tvíhendi øxina ok hjó til konungs, en konungrinn hvak undan lítt þat, ok missti kappinn hans ok hjó í jǫrðina niðr ok steypðisk eftir nǫkkvut svá, en konungrinn hjó hann með sverðinu í miðju í sundr í brynjunniᶜ svát sinn veg fell hvárr hlutrinn. En eftir þat er kempan var fallin, þá snørisk bardaginn á hendr þeim brœðrum, ok fellu þá þeir Gormr ok Erlingr í þeiriᵈ ok fjǫlði manna, en allir brœðr þeira flýðu til skipa ok svá ór landi, hverr sem komask mátti, en konungrinn Hǫkon rak flóttann með sínu liði. Þá flaug ǫr at konunginum, sú er engi vissi hverr skaut, ok fló undir brynstúkuna í arminn øfraᵉ í músina. En þat er sagt at með gørningum Gunnhildar snørisk matsveinn einnᶠ aftr með skeyti ok varð þetta á munni: 'Gefit rúm konungsbana!' ok lét fara skeytit í flokkinn er at móti fór, ok særði konunginn sem áðr sagði. En þá er konungrinn kenndi at þat var banasár, fyr því at hónum mátti eigi blóð stǫðva, þá bað hann konungrinn flytja sik til Alreksstaða, en á leiðinni koma þeir við hellu þá er nú heitirᵍ Hǫkonarhella. Þar hafði hann fœddr verit af ambǫtt þeiri er hét Þóra Morstǫng.ʰ Hón var af Most⟨r⟩ kynjuð ok fœdd, því var hón svá kǫlluð. En er konungrinn sá at at hónum leið, þá iðraðisk hann mjǫk mótgerða við guð. Vinir hans buðu hónum at fœra lík hans til Englands vestr ok jarða at kirkju.ⁱ 'Ek em eigi þess verðr,' kvað hann. 'Svá lifða ek

---

ᵃ here a word of about five letters has been erased; Storm suggested ǫðrum (Ágrip 1880, 103).

ᵇ hjálmaðr ok brynjaðr] added twice in the margin, once in the same hand, once in a younger hand.

ᶜ í brynjunni] added in the margin in the same hand.

ᵈ one expects here the word orrostu, but similar constructions occur elsewhere in the text and must be intentional.

ᵉ some, e. g. Bugge (1873, 8), have seen this as an error for hǫgra (i. e. hœgra, 'right').

ᶠ matsveinn einn] added in the margin in the same hand.

ᵍ written over the line is callloþ; previous editors have preferred this reading, although it requires the addition of er.

ʰ i. e. Mostrstǫng; this is perhaps simply an error.

ⁱ MS kirkiom, which scarcely makes sense.

Then the warrior strode forward, helmeted and mail-clad, and, gripping the axe with both hands, he struck at the king. The king drew back a little and the warrior missed him and struck the ground, stumbling somewhat. The king split him in two in the middle with his sword, through the chainmail, so that he fell in halves to either side.

When the champion had fallen, the tide of battle turned against the brothers, and then Gormr fell, and Erlingr, and many men besides. Their brothers all fled to ship and all who could left the country. But King Hákon and his forces pursued them. Then there flew toward the king an arrow—shot by no one knows whom—and it passed under the sleeve of his corselet and into the muscle of the upper arm. But it is said that through the sorcery of Gunnhildr a kitchen boy wheeled round, crying: 'Make room for the king's banesman!' and let fly the arrow into the group coming toward him and wounding the king, as has been said.

When the king realised that his wound was mortal—for the flow of blood could not be stopped—he asked to be moved to Alreksstaðir. Along the way they came to the slab of rock which is now called Hákonarhella. There he had been born of a bondwoman named Þóra Morstǫng. She was of Mostr-kin and had herself been born there and was for this reason so called.

When the king saw that death was near he repented greatly of his offences to God. His friends offered to take his body west to England and bury it there at a church. 'I am not worthy of that,' he said. 'I have lived in many ways

sem heiðnir menn í mǫrgu, skal mik ok fyr því svá jarða sem heiðna menn. Vætti ek mér þaðan af meiri miskunnar af guði sjǫlfum en ek sjá verðr,' ok andaðisk á Hǫkonarhellu, en[a] hann var heygðr á Sæheimi á Norðhǫrðalandi. Hann hǫrmuðu bæði vinir hans ok óvinir. Eigi var meira fé borit í haug með hónum en sverð hans Kvernbiti ok búnaðr hans. Í steinþró var hann lagðr í hauginum.

VII. En þat gǫrðisk þá umb Eiríks ævi blóðøxar er hann flýði ór landi at hann fluttisk með skipaliði vestr til Englands ok var í útilegu ok hernaði ok beiddisk miskunnar af Englands konungi, sem Aðalsteinn konungr hafði hónum heitit, en hann þá af konunginum jarlsríki á Norðimbralandi, gerðisk þar enn[b] með rǫ́ðum Gunnhildar konu sinnar svá grimmr ok greypr við lýð sinn at hann þóttisk varla bera mega. Af því réðsk hann í hernuð ok í víking víða í Vestrlandum, ok fell Eiríkr í Spáníalandi í útilegu. En Gunnhildr snørisk aftr til Danmarkar til Haralds konungs, er þá var konungr í Danmǫrku, ok var þar með sunu sína[c] til þess er þeir vǫ́ru rosknir menn mjǫk svá at aldri.

VIII. En eftir fráfall Hǫkonar tóku Norðmenn eftir ráði Hǫkonar konungs Harald gráfeld til konungs í Nóregi. En Haraldr gráfeldr kømr aftr í land ok náir ríki með brœðrum sínum Sigurði slefu, Goðrøði ljóma ok Ragnfrøði. Haraldr var þeira brœðra fremstr ok vænstr ok einna[d] bezt at sér gerr. Því var þetta kveðit —

    2. Æ standa mér augu
       of eld til Gráfeldar

—at maðrinn var[e] fríðr sýnum.

[a] added in the margin.
[b] MS er.
[c] sunu sína] apparently corrected from svnum sinum.
[d] added above the line, incorrectly after vænstr.
[e] added above the line.

as a heathen, and as a heathen shall I therefore be buried. I hope for greater mercy from God Himself than I am worthy of.' And he died at Hákonarhella and he was buried at Sæheimr in Norðhorðaland. He was mourned by both friends and enemies. There were no more goods set in his mound with him than his sword Kvernbiti and his battle-dress. He was laid in the mound in a stone coffin.

VII. And it happened then that when Eiríkr blóðøx fled the country he went west with his ships to England and there spent his time raiding and plundering. There he asked quarter of the English king, as Æthelstan had promised him.[31] He received from the king an earldom in Northumbria. Through the advice of his wife Gunnhildr he became once again so cruel and savage in his dealings with his people that they could scarcely endure it. Because of this he went raiding and harrying widely in western Europe and fell in Spain while on a raid.[32] Gunnhildr returned to King Haraldr, who was then king in Denmark, and remained there with her sons till they were fully grown to manhood.

VIII. After Hákon's death, the Norwegians, following King Hákon's counsel, took Haraldr gráfeldr as king in Norway. Haraldr gráfeldr returned to Norway and took the kingdom together with his brothers Sigurðr slefa, Guðrøðr ljómi and Ragnfrøðr. Haraldr was foremost of the brothers, the most accomplished and best looking. This verse was composed:

> 2. Steady is my eye across the fire
>   fixed on Grey-cloak;

because he was a handsome man.

IX. Haraldr [oooooooooooo][a] var konungr .x[v].[b] vetr. Hann fylgði rǫ́ðum móður sinnar ok gørði harðan rétt landsmanna ok þeir allir brœðr. Var um þeira ævi í Nóregi sultr ok seyra ok hverskyns illr yfirgangr. Þeir vǫ́ru allir ofstopamenn ok bardaga, vǫ́ru ok náliga allir fyr því drepnir at menn mǫ́ttu eigi þola þeim ofríki ok ólǫg. Svá er sagt at Vǫrsar gerðu fǫr at Haraldi konungi ok þeim brœðrum ok Sigurði[c] á þingi einu ok vildu taka af lífi, en þeir kómusk undan. En þeir drǫ́pu síðan[d] Sigurð slefu á Alreksstǫðum. Var þar flokksforingi Vémundr vǫlubrjótr. Drap [o][e] Sigurð maðr sá er hét Þorkell kleypr, er Sigurðr hafði tekit konu hans nauðga. Lagði hann Sigurð gegnum með sverði, ok hefndi hans þegar hirðmaðr hans, sá er hét Erlingr gamli. Haraldr gráfeldr g[erði fǫr at] Tr[yggva] brœðr[ung sínum ok drap hann], en Þórólfr lúsaskegg hljóp ór landi síðan með Óláf, son Tryggva konungs.[f]

X. Í þann tíð bauð Haraldr Danakonungr Haraldi gráfeld til sín af vél. Hann kom í Limafjǫrð þrim skipum, en þar kom á hendr hónum Gull-Haraldr, sunr Knúts, bróðursunr Haralds blátannar, með .ix. skipum, ok með ráðagørð þeira Hǫkonar jarls, er þá var jarl í Nóregi at fǫðurleif sinni síðan þeir brœðr réðu fǫður hans á Hǫklói í Þrǫ́ndheimi. En er Haraldr konungr gráfeldr sá at hann var svikum ok ofliði borinn, þá mælti hann við Gull-Harald: 'Þat hlœgir mik,' þá kvað hann,[g] 'at ek sé skamman þinn sigr, fyr því at Hǫkon jarl, frændi várr, ferr hér með liði ok drepr yðr á fœtr oss þegar ⟨á⟩ leið, ok hefnir svá vár.' Þar fell

[a] *the length of the erasure suggests there were probably two words here, the second of which may conceivably have been* gráfeldr; *Storm claimed to be able to make out* ldr (Ágrip 1880, 104).
[b] *the second letter is now impossible to read; the number could also be* .xii.
[c] ok Sigurði] *added above the line.*
[d] *added in the margin.*
[e] *here a single letter has been erased, probably* ħ (= hann).
[f] Haraldr . . . konungs] *this sentence is now largely unreadable, having been almost completely erased. The reconstruction derives from Storm* (Ágrip 1880, 105) *and has*

IX. Haraldr was king fifteen winters.[33] He followed his mother's counsel, and, with his brothers, tyrannised over the people. In their time there was hunger and starvation and injustices of every kind in Norway. They were all overbearing men, eager for battle, and nearly all were killed as a result of the fact that men would not suffer their tyranny and lawlessness.

It is said that the Vǫrsar rose against King Haraldr and the brothers and Sigurðr at an assembly and meant to kill them, but they escaped. But later they killed Sigurðr slefa at Alreksstaðir. There they were led by Vémundr vǫlubrjótr. Sigurðr was killed by a man named Þorkell kleypr,[34] whose wife he had forcibly taken. Þorkell ran him through with a sword, and one of Sigurðr's men called Erlingr gamli straightway avenged him.

Haraldr gráfeldr came against his cousin Tryggvi and killed him, but Þórólfr lúsarskegg fled the country with Óláfr, King Tryggvi's son.[35]

X. At that time Haraldr king of the Danes had treacherously invited Haraldr gráfeldr to Denmark. He sailed into Limafjǫrðr with three ships, and there Gull-Haraldr,[36] son of Knútr, nephew of Haraldr blátǫnn, came against him with nine ships, by the design of the Danish king and Jarl Hákon, who had become jarl of his patrimony in Norway after the brothers had killed his father at Hǫkló in Þrándheimr. But when King Haraldr gráfeldr saw that he had been betrayed and his forces outnumbered, he said to Gull-Haraldr: 'It makes me laugh,' he said, 'that I see your victory to be short-lived, because Jarl Hákon, my kinsman, is on his way here now with an army, and in killing you on our heels, he will straightway avenge us.'[37] King Haraldr gráfeldr

been accepted by every subsequent editor, but it is doubtful whether there would have been room in the line for both sínum *and* ok drap hann; *Storm read* vndan *for what appears rather to be* or landi. *The words* síðan *and* konungs *are added below the line.*

g þá kvað hann] *added, rather unnecessarily, in the margin.*

Haraldr konungr gráfeldr at Hálsi í Limafirði ok lið hans allt, en Hǫkon jarl drap þegar Gull-Harald ok vann svá Nóreg undir sik, með skattgildi við Danakonung.

XI. En eftir fráfall Haralds kømr Hǫkon jarl til ríkis ok hafði einn Nóreg allan mjǫk svá, ok undir jarls nafni sem hans forellrar hǫfðu haft. Ætt hans var af Hǫleygjum ok af Mœrum, ok jarla ætt í hvára tveggja kvísl, ok vildi hann fyrir því eigi tígna sik konungs nafni. Faðir hans hét Sigurðr Hyrnajarl en móðir hans Bergljót, dóttir Þóris þegjanda, jars[a] af Mœri. Hann átti Ólofu, dóttur Haralds hárfagra. Hón var móðir Bergljótar. Hann hafði enn at nýfengnu ríki gagnstǫðu í fyrstunni af Gunnhildi konungamóður, ok lá hvárt umb annat með illum prettum, þvíat þat skorti hvárki þeira. Hǫkon jarl var manna vænstr sýnum, ekki hǫr, [ooooooo][b] virðiligr. Hann var spekingr mikill í vizku sinni, ok varð hann fyr því slœgri en Gunnhildr í sínum rǫðum. Hann átti enn vingótt við Harald konung, er þá réð fyr Danmǫrku, ok bœndi hann til at hann skyldi koma flárǫðum við Gunnhildi, ok koma henni ór landi með þeim hætti at hann sendi henni rit sitt ok sendi menn at biðja hennar. Ok hann sendi henni rit ok kvað þat sœmst at hón gǫmul giftisk gǫmlum konungi, ok hón hlýddi á þat, ok var hennar fǫr ger prýðiliga til óprúðar,[c] þvíat þegar hón kom til Danmarkar þá var hón tekin ok søkkt í mýri einni, ok lauk svá hón[d] sínum dǫgum, at því sem margir segja.

XII. En Hǫkon jarl sat í ríki .xx. vetr síz Haraldr gráfeldr fell at Hálsi í Limafirði, ok sat með ríki miklu ok óvinsæl⟨d⟩[e]

---

[a] *i. e.* jarls; *see Noreen 1923, § 291.7.*

[b] *here a word of about seven letters has been erased; in the margin the word* riþuaxinn *has been added in a slightly younger hand.*

[c] prýðilega til óprúðar] *written* prvþþilega til opprvþar. *While the meaning is fairly obvious, the syntax of this sentence is not immediately clear; there appears to be an omission or error, or both. Most previous editors (e. g. Finnur Jónsson, Ágrip 1929, 15) have emended to* óprúðrar, *following which the word* farar *is to be understood. Another possibility, however, is that a construction such as* varð (henni) til óprýði *is meant, either with an otherwise unattested gen. sg.* prýðar (*cf. Noreen 1923, § 411.2*), *or a gen.*

fell there, at Háls in Limafjǫrðr, and all his men, but Hákon immediately killed Gull-Haraldr, winning Norway for himself as a vassal of the Danish king.

XI. Following the death of Haraldr, Jarl Hákon came to power and ruled alone very nearly all Norway, and with the jarl's title his forefathers had had. His kin were Háleygir and Mœrir, and there had been jarls on both sides, for which reason he did not wish to honour himself by assuming the kingly title. His father was called Sigurðr Hyrnajarl, and his mother was Bergljót, the daughter of Þórir þegjandi, jarl of Mœrr. He was married to Ólof, daughter of Haraldr hárfagri. She was Bergljót's mother.

In the early days of his reign Hákon had opposition from Gunnhildr konungamóðir,[38] and they were often engaged in nasty trickery each against the other, for neither of them was lacking in that.

Jarl Hákon was the handsomest of men, not tall, but imposing. He was a man of great wisdom and therefore more cunning than Gunnhildr in his machinations. He was then still on good terms with King Haraldr, who then ruled Denmark, and asked him to trick Gunnhildr into leaving the country by sending to her messengers bearing a writ proffering marriage. And Haraldr sent her the writ, saying it would be fitting that she in her old age marry an old king, and she agreed to do this. But her journey, which began in splendour, ended in disgrace, for when she arrived in Denmark she was taken and sunk in a bog, and, according to many, so ended her days.[39]

XII. Hákon jarl ruled twenty winters after the death of Haraldr gráfeldr at Háls in Limafjǫrðr. He ruled imperiously, and, as time passed, grew more and more unpopular, particu-

prúðar *from a nom.* prúðr (*cf. Noreen 1923, § 384 and Anm. 1*).
  [d] svá hón] hón svá *would be more natural.*
  [e] *cf. p. 48; also* vinsæld, *pp. 10 and 70, and* óvinsæld, *p. 46.*

mikilli ok margfaldri, er á leið upp, ok með einni þeiri er hann dró til heljar, at hann lét sér konur allar jamt heimilar er hann fýsti til, ok var engi kvenna munr í því gǫrr, ok engi grein, hvers kona hver væri, eða systir, eða dóttir.

XIII. En hann fýsti eitthvert sinni til konu þeirar er Guðrún hét Lundasól. Hón bjó á Lundum í Gauladali,[a] ok gerði hann af Meðalhúsum þræla sína at taka hana ok flytja sér til ósœmðar. En meðan þrælarnir mǫtuðusk, þá hafði hón svá liði safnat at þá var eigi kostr at flytja hana, ok sendi hón þá orð Hǫkoni jarli at hón mundi eigi á hans fund sœkja, nema hann[b] sendi konu þá er hann hafði er Þóra hét á Remoli. En eftir þau orð sœkir hann upp í Gauladal með ǫllu liði sínu. En Halldórr á Skerðingssteðju skar upp ǫr allt at dalinum, ok sótti alla vega flokkr á mót hónum. Ok þá er jarlinn sá liðit, ok hann fann at hann var svikinn, þá dreifði hann ǫllu liði sínu frá sér. En hann ok þræll hans Karkr[c] riðu vakar nekkurar ok drekkðu þar hesti hans ok létu eftir skikkju hans ok svá sverð á ísinum, en þeir fluttusk í helli einn er enn heitir Jarlshellir í Gauladali. Ok sofnaði þar þrællinn, ok lét illa, ok sagði síðan, er hann vaknaði, at maðr svartr ok ililigr fór hjá hellinum, ok óttaðisk hann at hann mundi inn ganga, ok sagði hónum at Ulli var drepinn. En jarlinn svaraði at þá myndi vera drepinn sunr hans, ok svá varð ok. Sofnar þrællinn í annat sinni, ok lætr eigi betr en fyrr, sagði síðan at inn sami maðr hafði þá farit ofan aftr, ok bað segja jarlinum at þá vǫru lokin sund ǫll. En jarlinn skildi í því kominn endadag sinn, ok fluttisk til Remols til konu þeirar er Þóra hét, er var friðla hans, ok hón leyndi hónum ok þrælinum í svínstí sínu. Síðan kom flokkr ok rannsakaði, ok með því at hann fannsk eigi, þá ætlaðisk flokkrinn at brenna bœinn upp at

---

[a] *first written* golar-, *but with the* o *corrected to* au *and the* r *erased.*
[b] *MS* hon.
[c] *MS* carki, *presumably an error.*

larly because—and this led to his death—he considered all women whom he desired equally available to him, making no distinction as to who was whose wife or sister or daughter.

XIII. He once desired a woman named Guðrún Lundasól. She lived at Lundir in Gauladalr, and he sent his thralls from Meðalhús to get her and bring her to him for unseemly purposes. But while the thralls were eating she got together so great a band of men that there was no possibility of taking her. She sent word to Jarl Hákon saying that she would not seek his company unless he sent away the woman he kept as mistress, who was named Þóra of Remol. After these words he proceeded to Gauladalr with all his men.

Halldórr of Skerðingssteðja called men to arms from everywhere in the valley, and a band of men came against the jarl from every direction. When the jarl saw the forces and realised that he had been betrayed, he sent away all his men and he and his thrall Karkr[40] rode till they came to a hole in the ice, and there they drowned his horse and laid his cloak and then his sword on the ice, and then they went to a cave, which is still called Jarlshellir, in Gauladalr.

There the thrall fell asleep and rested uneasily and said afterwards when he awoke that a man dark and grim had passed before the cave, and he had feared that the man would enter. Then he had told him that Ulli was dead. The jarl answered that his son must then be slain, and this was so.[41] The thrall slept again and rested no better than before, saying afterwards that the same man had passed again and had asked him to tell the jarl that all hope was gone.[42] And the jarl understood from this that his last day was come, and they went to Remol, to the woman named Þóra, who was his mistress,[43] and she hid him and the thrall in her pig-sty.

Later a band of men came and searched the house, and finding nothing, they intended to burn the farm to the

hringum. En þá er jarlinn heyrði þat, þá vildi hann eigi bíða písla af óvinum sínum, ok lét þrælinn skera sik á barka, ok lauk svá saurlífismaðr í saurgu húsi sínum dǫgum, ok svá ríki. Var hǫfuðit flutt til Kaupangs. Ok þá er liðit fór ofan of Steinbjǫrg, þá var fjǫrðrinn allr fullr af skipum, er allr lýðrinn sótti eftir ǫru hann af lífi at taka. Var þá hǫfuðit flutt í Hólm, ok kastaði hverr maðr steini at, en þrællinn Karkr bar í ljós hǫfuðit ok vænti sér af því lífs, en hann var þó upp hengðr. Þat vas of vár er Hǫkon dó. Í því bili kom Óláfr Tryggvasunr af Englandi í Nóreg [ooooooooooooooooooooo].[a] En Eiríkr Hǫkonarsunr stǫkk ór landi [ooooooo] ok fór til handa Óláfi enum sœnska í Svíþjóð, ok þeir Sveinn bróðir hans.

XIV. ⟨E⟩n Hǫkon jarl réð eigi firir því einn fyr Nóregi at hann ætti eftir þá at taka er næst hǫfðu áðr fyrir hónum konungar verit, nema fyrir styrks sakar ok megins, ok at hann var vitr maðr, þóat hann snøri viti sínu til ills, ok fyrir þess annars sakar at ætt ǫll Gunnhildarsuna var þá farin ok sløkkð náliga, ok þóat hón væri nǫkkur, þá var ǫllum mǫnnum á henni hatr ok vænti sér þá betra, ok gafsk vǫn at lygi.

XV. ⟨E⟩n hann átti þó ætterni til konungs þess at telja langfeðgum er Hersir hét. Hann var konungr í Naumudali. Hét kona hans Vigða, er enn heitir ǫin eftir Vigða í Naumudali. En Hersir missti hennar ok vildi týna sér eftir hana, ef dœmi fyndis⟨k⟩ til at þat hefði nekkverr konungr fyrri gǫrt. En dœmi fundusk til at jarl hefði þat gǫrt, en eigi at konungr hefði þat gǫrt. Ok hann fór þá á haug nekkvern ok veltisk fyrir ofan, ok kvaðsk þá hafa velzk ór konungs nafni, ok hengði sik síðan í jarls nafni, ok vildi hans afspringr síðan ávallt eigi við konungs nafni taka. En

[a] *here approximately a line and a half of text (4.7 cm) has been erased.*

ground. When the jarl heard this he wished not to be tortured by his enemies and had the thrall slit his throat,[44] and thus a man who had lived a life of filth ended, in a house of filth, his days and his rule. The head was taken to Kaupangr. And when the men came down from Steinbjǫrg the fjord was full of ships, as all the people had received the call to battle, so Hákon's life could be taken.[45]

The head was then moved to Hólmr, and there every man threw a stone at it. The thrall Karkr had come forward with the head, and for this he expected to be given his life, but he was hanged nevertheless.[46] It was in the spring that Hákon died.

At that same time Óláfr Tryggvason came to Norway from England. Eiríkr Hákonarson fled the country to Sweden with his brother Sveinn, and there they joined Óláfr the Swede.

XIV. Jarl Hákon had not ruled alone over Norway through right of descent from those who had been kings before him, but rather as a result of strength and force, and because he was a wise man, though he turned his wisdom to evil; and furthermore because the sons of Gunnhildr and their kin were all gone and had nearly all been killed, and though there were some of their kin, all men hated them, and had hoped for better, though they hoped in vain.

XV. Yet he had had, among his ancestors, a king whose name was Hersir. He had been king in Naumudalr. His wife was called Vigða and the river in Naumudalr is still called Vigða after her.[47] Hersir suffered her loss and wished to kill himself after her if an instance could be found of a king having done this before. It was found that a jarl had done so, but never a king. He went then to the top of a mound and rolled down, saying he had thus rolled from the kingship, and then he hanged himself as a jarl and for this reason his descendants would afterwards never take the

sǫnnendi[a] til þessa má heyra í Hǫ́leygjatali er Eyvindr orti, er kallaðr var skáldaspillir.

XVI. ⟨E⟩n til ríkis eftir Hǫ́kon jarl steig Óláfr Tryggvasunr, ok tígnaði sik konungs nafni í Nóregi, er ættar rétt átti af Haraldi hárfagra, þvíat Óláfr hét sunr Haralds, er faðir var Tryggva, er of daga Gunnhildarsuna tók konungs nafn ok vald á Raumaríki, ok var þar tekinn af lífi á Sótanesi ok er þar heygðr, ok kalla menn þar[b] Tryggvareyr. En aftak hans segja eigi allir einum hætti. Sumir kenna búǫndum, at þeim þótti yfirboð hans hart ok drópu hann á þingi. Sumir segja at hann skyldi gera sætt við fǫðurbróðursunu sína, ok tóku þeir hann af með svikum ok illræðum Gunnhildar konungamóður, ok trúa því flestir.

XVII. ⟨E⟩n eftir fráfall hans þá flýði Estríð,[c] er Tryggvi hafði fengit á Upplǫndum, braut til Orkneyja með Óláfi þrévetrum, syni sínum ok Tryggva, at forðask bæði fláræði Gunnhildar ok suna hennar ok Hǫ́konar jarls, er ǫll kippðusk þá enn[d] um Nóreg, þvíat eigi vǫru þá enn synir Gunnhildar af lífi teknir. Ok kom hón til Orkneyja með þrimr skipsǫgnum. En með því at eigi mátti leynask ferð hennar, ok mart kunni til svika gerask, þá sendi hón barnit á braut með manni þeim er sumir kalla Þórólf lúsarskegg [ooooooooooo],[e] ok hafði hann barnit á launungu á braut til Nóregs, ok flutti með miklum ótta til Svíþjóðar. Ok ór Svíþjóð[f] vildi hann fara til Hólmgarðs, þvíat þar var nǫkkvut ætterni hans. En þá kvǫ́mu Eistr at skipi því er hann var á, ok var sumt[g] drepit af, en sumt hertekit, fóstri hans drepinn, en hann hertekinn fyr ey þeiri er heitir Eysýsla, en síðan seldr í nauð.

[a] *written* sa/nnendi; *perhaps simply an error for* sannendi.
[b] *added above the line.*
[c] *written* æstriþ, *the Danish form of* Ástríðr.
[d] *added above the line.*
[e] *here Storm read* sumir loþskeggi (Ágrip *1880, 108*).
[f] *MS* sviþior.
[g] *written here and four words on* sumpt.

name of king. The truth of this can be heard in the Háleygjatal, which Eyvindr composed, who was called skáldaspillir.[48]

XVI. After Hákon jarl Óláfr Tryggvason ascended the throne and assumed the name of king in Norway, to which he had right through descent from Haraldr hárfagri, because one of Haraldr's sons was named Óláfr, who was the father of Tryggvi, who in the days of the sons of Gunnhildr held the title and authority of king in Raumaríki. He was killed on Sótanes and there buried and men call this place Tryggvareyrr.[49] But not all tell of his slaying in the same way: some blame the farmers, that they felt his rule to be harsh and killed him at assembly; some say that he was about to be reconciled with his cousins, and that they killed him through the treachery and wicked counsel of Gunnhildr konungamóðir, and most believe this.

XVII. After his death, Ástríðr, whom Tryggvi had married in Upplǫnd, fled to Orkney with Óláfr, their three-year-old son,[50] in order to avoid both the treachery of Gunnhildr and her sons and that of Jarl Hákon, who were all still struggling for control of Norway, for the sons of Gunnhildr had not yet been slain. Ástríðr came to Orkney with three fully-manned ships, but because her voyage could not be concealed and much perfidy could befall them, she sent the child away with the man whom some call Þórólfr lúsarskegg.[51] He took the child in secrecy to Norway and thence, in great fear, to Sweden. He wished to go from Sweden to Hólmgarðr, for some of Óláfr's kin were there.[52] Men from Estonia came on board their ship and killed some men and took others hostage. Þórólfr was killed and Óláfr taken hostage near the island called Eysýsla,[53] and afterwards sold into slavery.

XVIII. ⟨E⟩n guð, er þetta barn hafði kosit til stórra hluta, stillti hónum til lausnar með þeim hætti at maðr kom til Eistlands, sendimaðr konungs af Hólmgarði, er var sendr at taka skatt af landinu, ok var frændi barnsins ok leysti frænda sinn ok hafði til Hólmgarðs, ok var hann þar umb hríð svá at ekki var margra manna vitorð á hans ætterni. En þá er hann var .xij. vetra gamall, þá gerðisk svá til at um dag nekkvern á torgi, þá kenndi hann í hendi manni øxi þá er Þórólfr hafði haft, ok leitaði eftir atburðum hvé hónum hefði sú øx komit, ok varð af hins ansvǫrum sannfróðr at þat var bæði øx fóstra hans ok svá bani, ok tók øxina ór hendi hónum ok drap þann er þangat hafði, ok hefndi svá fóstra síns. En þar var mannhelgr mikil ok miklar viðlǫgur við manns aftak, ok fekk hann þat til ráðs at hann hljóp á hald dróttningarinnar, ok með bœn hennar, ok af því at hvatligt þótti vera verkit manni .xij. vetra gǫmlum at vinna, ok af því at sannlig þótti hefndin vera, þá þá hann miskunn af konunginum, ok tók síðan at vaxa vitorð of hann ok svá metorð ok allt yfirlæti. En síðan er á leið á stundina, þá var hónum fengit lið ok skipastóll, ok fór hann bæði á eitt land[a] ok ǫnnur lǫnd ok herjaði, ok aukuðu flokk hans brátt Norðmenn ok Gautar ok Danir, ok vann nú stórvirki, ok aflaði sér með því frægðar ok góðs orðlags.

XIX. ⟨H⟩ann drýgði víða herskap bæði á Vendlandi[b] ok á Flæmingjalandi, á Englandi ok á Skotlandi, á Írlandi ok á mǫrgum ǫðrum lǫndum, hafði iðuliga vetrsetu sína á Vennlandi í borg þeiri er hét Jómsborg. En hvégi lengi sem hann drýgði slíkt athæfi, þá gørðisk svá til of síðir at hann lendi þar við í einum stað í Englandi sem var einn mikill guðs vinr ok sá einsetumaðr ok frægr af góðum vísendum

[a] *MS á eít land, with* o *added above the* a (= lǫnd); *Brieskorn (1909, 147–48) suggests this should be read á* Eistlǫnd, *the plural being used to refer to the area covered by the present-day Baltic republics.*

[b] *Dahlerup (Ágrip 1880, 109) suggests emending to* frislande, *and Bugge (1873, 9) adding* oc a frislande.

XVIII. But God, who had chosen this child for great things, saw to his release in this way: a man came to Estonia, an ambassador from the king in Hólmgarðr, sent to collect tribute in that country. He was the child's kinsman, and he ransomed his kinsman and brought him to Hólmgarðr. There he remained a while and few knew of his descent.

When he was twelve years old,[54] it happened one day in the market place that he recognised in a man's hand the axe Þórólfr had had, and he asked the man under what circumstances he had come to possess the axe. From his answers Óláfr knew for certain that this was both his fosterfather's axe and also his slayer. He took the axe from his hands and killed him who had brought it there, thus avenging his fosterfather.

Inviolability of the person was there highly regarded, and there were great penalties for manslaughter, and Óláfr resolved then to seek the support of the queen. Through her petition and because it was thought a manly deed for a twelve-year-old to have performed—and because it was considered a just revenge—he was granted the king's pardon. Thereafter, as report of him increased, so also did his esteem and honour. And as time went on he was given men and ships and went harrying from land to land. Norwegians, Gauts[55] and Danes quickly swelled his flock, and through great feats he won for himself fame and good repute.

XIX. He harried widely, both in Wendland and Flanders, in England and in Scotland, in Ireland and in many other countries,[56] generally wintering in Wendland, in the town called Jómsborg.[57] But however long he kept up such practice, it happened finally that he came to a place in England[58] where there lived a great man of God, a hermit, famed for good and wide learning. Óláfr wished to test

ok margfróðum. Ok fýstisk Óláfr at freista þess ok gerði einn sinn þjónustumann í konungs búnaði hans hjálpræða at leita sér undir konungs nafni, ok fekk þessur ansvǫr: 'Eigi ertu konungr, en þat er ráð mitt attu sér trúr konungi þínum.' Ok fýsti Óláf ok at meirr hann at finna er hann hafði heyrt slík andsvǫr, þvíat nú tók ím af hónum at hann var sannr própheti. En í hans viðrtalan ok þess ens góða manns fortǫlu, þá mælti hann við hann með þessum orðum af heilagri vitrun ok hifneskri framsýn: 'Þú mont vera,' kvað hann, 'ágætr konungr ok ágæt verk vinna. Þú munt mǫrgum þjóðum til trúar koma ok til skírnar, montu bæði þér í því ok svá mǫrgum ǫðrum hjálpa. Ok til þess attu ifisk eigi um þessur mín ansvǫr, þá montu þetta til marks hafa: þú munt við skip þín svikum mœta ok flokkum, ok mon á bardaga reitask, ok montu týna nǫkkvuru liði ok sjálfr sár fá, ok montu af því sári banvænn vera ok á skildi til skips borinn. En af þessu sári montu heill verða ⟨i⟩nnan .vij. nátta, ok brátt eftir þat við skírn taka.' Allt gekksk eftir þessi sǫgu, ok kom hann svá til trúar, því næst til Nóregs, ok hafði með sér Sigurð byskup, er til þess var vígðr at boða lýðum guðs nafn, ok enn nekkvera lærða menn, Þangbrand prest ok Þormóð, ok enn nekkver djǫkn. Ok of kristnis boð kom hann fysta þingi á í Mostr á Hǫrðulandi, ok var auðvelt at flytja, bæði at guð studdi ok mǫnnum hafði verit leið áþján Hǫkonar illa, ok tók þar[a] lýðr við trú, en Óláfr við ríki. Hann hafði .vij. vetr ok .xx. er hann kom í Nóreg, ok á þeim .v. vetrum er hann bar konungs nafn í Nóregi krisnaði[b] hann .v. lǫnd: Nóreg ok Ísland ok Hjaltland, Ork⟨n⟩eyjar ok it .v.[c] Færeyjar, ok reisti fyrst kirkjur á sjálf⟨s⟩ síns hǫfuðbólum, ok felldi blót ok blótdrykkjur, ok lét í stað koma í vild við lýðinn

[a] MS þ (*i. e.* þat).
[b] *i. e.* kristnaði, *cf. below, pp. 34 and 74*.
[c] *first written* vj, *but the* j *has been erased*.

him and sent one of his retainers dressed in kingly clothing to seek helping advice in the name of king, and he received this answer: 'You are no king, but it is my advice that you be loyal to your king.' And when Óláfr heard such an answer he desired even more to meet him, for now he was in no doubt that he was a true prophet.[59] In the course of that good man's conversation and persuasion he spoke to Óláfr with these words of holy revelation and heavenly foresight: 'You will be,' he said, 'an excellent king and do excellent works, and you will bring many peoples to faith and baptism, and in this way you will benefit both yourself and many others. And so that you may not doubt my words, you shall take this as a sign: at your ships you will meet with treachery and bands of men. It will end in battle and you will lose some of your men and you yourself be wounded. As a result of this wound you will be near death, and you will be borne on a shield to your ship. But from this wound you will recover within seven nights, and soon afterward you will receive baptism.'[60] All happened as had been told, and in this way Óláfr came to the faith and then to Norway, and brought with him Bishop Sigurðr, who had been ordained to proclaim the name of God to the people; and still other learned men, the priest Þangbrandr and Þormóðr[61] and also several deacons. He first proclaimed the Christian faith at an assembly at Mostr in Hǫrðaland—and it was easy to preach, both because it was supported by God and because men had grown tired of the tyranny of Hákon illi[62]—and there the people took the faith and Óláfr the kingdom.

He was twenty-seven years old when he came to Norway,[63] and during the five years he bore the name of king in Norway he Christianised five countries: Norway, Iceland, Shetland, Orkney and the fifth, the Faeroes.[64] He first raised churches on his own estates and he abolished pagan feasts and sacrifices, in place of which, as a favour

hótíðardrykkjur jól ok páskar, Jóansmessu mungát, ok haustǫl at Míkjálsmessu. Óláfr var mikill maðr, hár, sýniligr, hvítr á hárslit allan[a], rétthærðr ok manna snøriligastr ok bezt at sér gǫrr í allri korteisi.

XX. ⟨E⟩n brátt eftir þetta kvángaðisk Óláfr ok tók systur Sveins tjúguskeggs Danakonungs, er Þyri hét, er hertogi nekkverr í Vinnlandi hafði festa[b] nauðga, ok heldusk fyr því eigi þau festarmǫl. En eftir samkvǫmu þeira þá veitti Sveinn konungr áhald þingum þeim er ját vǫru, ok skilat með systur hans, ok þótti Óláfi konungi sú neisa með sneypu. Ok at hefna þess þá safnaði hann her til Danmarkar ok beið liðsins í landamæri, ok með því at seinkaðisk kváma þeira, þá helt hann yfir til Vinðlands með .xi. einum skipum ok vænti liðs eftir sér. En þá er sú vǫn varð at lygi—af því at flokkrinn vendi þegar aftr, er hann var ór landi—þá ætlaðisk hann at afla sér gengis í Vinðlandi af sínum sannvinum, er hónum hǫfðu í útilegu hollir vinir verit ok tryggvir félagar. En þat tósk[c] eigi, þvíat Sveinn konungr hafði kvatt til liðs með sér Óláf Svíakonung ok Eirík, sun Hǫkonar illa, ok kvǫmu þessir at hónum fyrir Sjólandi með tveim[d] skipum ok átta tøgum skipa. Sveinn hafði .xxx. skipa ok Óláfr .xxx. skipa, Eiríkr .ii. ok .xx., ok lagði at hónum fyrst Sveinn með .xxx. skipa, ok fór manntjón mikla, ok vendi aftr með sneypu. En því næst lagði til Óláfr enn svenski með jǫfnu liði við Svein, ok bar aftr jafna sneypu. Síðan lagði Eiríkr at ok bar øfra skjǫld. En til falls Óláfs konungs var ekki vitat. Hitt var sét, at þá er mjǫk rénaði orrostan, at hann stóð lífs þá enn í lyftinginni á Orminum langa, er hafði tvau rúm ok .xxx. En þá er Eiríkr skyldi ganga upp í stafninn á leit hans, þá sleri ljósi fyrir hann sem elding væri, en konungrinn sjálfr horfinn er

[a] á hárslit allan] *written in a slightly younger hand over an erasure.*
[b] *following this word an* s *has been written, but partially erased.*
[c] *i. e.* tóksk.
[d] tveim] *written* tvém *or* tvéin.

to the people, he ordained the holiday feasts Yule and Easter, St John's Mass ale and an autumn-ale at Michaelmas.

Óláfr was a big man, tall and handsome, with straight, light hair and beard, and of all men he was the quickest and best versed in all courtly behaviour.

XX. Soon after this Óláfr married the sister of Sveinn tjúguskegg, king of the Danes, whose name was Þyri and whom a duke in Wendland had forcibly betrothed to himself, for which reason the betrothal had not stood.[65]

After the wedding King Sveinn withheld the things promised in dowry with his sister, and King Óláfr considered this a disgrace. To seek vengeance he collected an army to go to Denmark and awaited forces on the coast,[66] but because their arrival was delayed, he sailed to Wendland with only eleven ships, expecting the army to follow him. But when his hope was not realised, because the men had turned back as soon as he was out of the country, he intended to gather support in Wendland among his true friends, who had been faithful friends and trusted companions with him on viking expeditions. But this proved unsuccessful, for King Sveinn had called upon Óláfr, King of the Swedes, and Eiríkr, son of Hákon illi, and they came against him off Sjóland with eighty-two ships: Sveinn had thirty ships, Óláfr thirty and Eiríkr twenty-two. Sveinn came first against him with thirty ships, but suffered great losses and turned back with disgrace. Then came Óláfr the Swede with equal strength, and he met with equal disgrace. Lastly came Eiríkr and he won the day.[67]

But of the fall of King Óláfr nothing was known. It was seen that as the fighting lessened he stood, still alive, on the high-deck astern on the Long Serpent, which had thirty-two rowing-places.[68] But when Eiríkr went to the stern of the ship in search of the king, a light flashed before him, as though it were lightning, and when the light disap-

ljósit hvarf af. Sumir menn geta hann á báti braut hafa komizk, ok segja at hann hafi verit sénn síðan í munklífi nǫkkvuru á Jórsalalandi. En sumir geta at hann hafi fyrir borð fallit. En hvatki er lífi hans hefir lukt, þá er þat líkiligt at guð hafi sǫ́lina.

XXI. ⟨E⟩n með því at Sveini þótti þá sem hann hefði unnit Nóreg með aftaki Óláfs, þá játti hann Eiríki ok Sveini, sunum Hǫkonar, Nóregi, ok helt Eiríkr einn landi síðan Sveinn fell á frá, Danakonungr. Ok þá er Eiríkr hafði alls stýrt Nóregi .xii. vetr með jarls nafni, þá gaf hann upp Hǫkoni syni sínum landit, en hann fór til Englands vestr ok réðsk í lið með Knúti, mági sínum, er hann vann England, ok dó þar af blóðrǫ́s er hónum var úfr skorinn.

XXII. ⟨E⟩n svá mikla kostan ok stund sem Óláfr Tryggvasunr lagði á at fremja krisni[a]—er við ekki vétta sparðisk,[b] þat er guði væri tígn í ok kristninni styrkr—svá lǫgðu þeir feðgar allt megin fram at drekkja kristninni, ok svá[c] gæfisk, ef eigi hefði guð þá sína miskunn til sent með tilkvǫmu Óláfs ⟨Haraldssunar⟩ grœnska, er þat mund hafði hug sinn mjǫk á veraldar sigri, sem hér má brátt heyra, ok veik síðan trú sinni til kristni ok laut af staðfestu trúar eilífa sælu ok helgi. En at menn viti ætterni hans til ríkis, þá má hér nú heyra.

XXIII. ⟨H⟩araldr, faðir Óláfs ens helga, hann var sunr Guðrøðar, en Guðrøðr sunr Bjarnar, en Bjǫrn sunr Haralds hárfagra, er fyrsti einvaldskonungr var yfir Nóregi. En mart er sagt frá víðlendi ferðar Óláfs, en hvégi víða er hann fór, þá sótti hann þegar aft⟨r⟩ er guð vildi opna ríki fyrir hónum, ok kom hann siglandi vestan af Englandi með

---

[a] *i. e.* kristni.

[b] written sparþist. *If this is not simply a scribal error* (t *for* c) *it is among the earliest examples of the later medio-passive ending* -st *in Icelandic; even so it may derive from the exemplar. See Kjartan G. Ottósson 1992, 93.*

[c] *added in the margin.*

peared, the king himself was gone. Some suppose he got away in a boat and say that he was seen afterwards in a monastery in the Holy Land, but others think that he fell overboard. But whatever ended his life, it is likely that God has the soul.

XXI. Because Sveinn felt that he had won Norway through Óláfr's death he granted it to Eiríkr and Sveinn, Jarl Hákon's sons,[69] and Eiríkr ruled the country alone after King Sveinn of Denmark died.[70] And when Eiríkr had ruled Norway twelve winters in all with the title of jarl, he left the country to his son Hákon and went west to England,[71] where he took service in the army of his brother-in-law Knútr,[72] when he conquered England, and there bled to death when his uvula was cut.[73]

XXII. But as much pain and effort as Óláfr Tryggvason had put into forwarding Christianity—and he spared nothing which was to the honour of God and the strengthening of the Christian faith—so Eiríkr and his son put all their strength into the quelling of it; and this would have come to pass had not God's mercy been manifested in the arrival of Óláfr, son of Haraldr grenski,[74] who at that time had his mind much set on worldly victory, as will soon be heard.[75] He later turned his faith to Christianity and through his steadfast belief gained eternal bliss and sanctity.

And that men may know of his ancestral birthright to the realm, this may now be heard.

XXIII. Haraldr, father of St Óláfr, was the son of Guðrøðr, and Guðrøðr the son of Bjǫrn, and Bjǫrn the son of Haraldr hárfagri, who was the first sole monarch of Norway.

Much is said about the extent of Óláfr's travels, but however widely he travelled, he returned when God wished to make the kingdom available to him,[76] and he came from

knǫrrum tveim, ok kom at við Sælu ok sigldi síðan í Sauðungasund. Ok svá sem guð skipaði til, þá var sén fǫr Hǫkonar, er þá stýrði landi eftir Eirík fǫður sinn, .xv. vetra gamall, enn vænsti maðr, ok stefndi í Sauðungasund, sem allra manna leið var í þat mund, ok óvitandi at Óláfr digri lá fyrir, ok hafði eigi Hǫkon lið meira en langskip eitt ok skútu eina. En þá er konungrinn varð varr við ferð hans, lagði hann sínu megin sundsins hvǫru skipinu. En þá er Hǫkon røri á þá, heimtusk brátt skip hans saman, ok varð hann þar hantekinn[a], ok þá hann líf ok svá lið hans allt af konunginum, ok fyrsvór landit Nóreg Óláfi eilífliga. Þá hǫfðu þeir feðgar Eiríkr ok Hǫkon landi ráðit .xiiij. vetr með jarls nafni ok Sveinn Hǫkonarsunr. Enn helgi Óláfr gaf hónum Hǫkoni Suðreyjar, sem sumir segja, ok styrkði hann svá at þeira var hann halzi ok þar var hann konungr meðan hann lifði.

XXIV. ⟨E⟩n þá tók inn helgi Óláfr við Nóregs ríki ok styrkði ríki sitt með kristni ok ǫllum góðum siðum, ok bar þó með mikilli óhœgð, þvíat margir leituðu á innan lands ok útan, allra helzt fyr kristnis sakar er hann bauð. Hann var enn fyrsta vetr lengstum með Sigurði mági sínum á Upplǫndum, en of várit eftir sótti Sveinn jarl með herskildi í land hans, ok heldu orrostu fyr Nesjum pálmadag við Grenmar, ok vann Óláfr sigr. Þar fell mikill hlutr lið⟨s⟩ Sveins, en Sveinn helt undan. Einarr þambaskelmir kastaði akkeri í skip Sveins ok sigldi með hann nauðgan á braut til Danmarkar. Síðan fór Sveinn austr í Garða, ok kom aldregi aftr.

XXV. ⟨S⟩íðan bað Óláfr dóttur Óláfs sœnska, Ástríðar, systur Ingigerðar,[b] er fyrr var heitin hónum, ok brá faðir

---

[a] i. e. handtekinn; cf. p. 56.
[b] MS ingi riþar.

the west, sailing from England with two ships, and made land at Sæla and then sailed into Sauðungasund.

And as God had ordained, Hákon's approach could be seen—fifteen years old and a very handsome man, he then ruled the country after his father Eiríkr—and he headed for Sauðungasund, at that time a common route, and was unaware that Óláfr digri lay ahead. He had no more forces than one longship and a small cutter. When the king realised that Hákon was coming, he placed his ships one on either side of the strait. And when Hákon rowed up to them, his ships immediately pulled towards each other and Hákon was there taken captive.[77] He and all his men were granted life by the king, and Hákon pledged Norway to Óláfr for all time.

Eiríkr and his son Hákon had then ruled Norway for fourteen years with a jarl's title, together with Sveinn Hákonarson. St Óláfr gave Hákon the Hebrides, according to some, and supported him so that he was able to keep them, and he was king there for as long as he lived.[78]

XXIV. And so St Óláfr became king of Norway and strengthened his kingdom through Christianity and good ways, although with great difficulty, for there were many who opposed him, both within and without Norway, particularly because of the Christian faith he preached.

He spent most of the first winter with his stepfather Sigurðr in Upplǫnd.[79] The following spring Jarl Sveinn attacked the country and they met in battle on Palm Sunday off Nesjar by Grenmarr and the victory was Óláfr's.[80] There fell a great part of Sveinn's army, but Sveinn himself escaped. Einarr þambarskelmir[81] cast an anchor onto Sveinn's ship and forced him to sail away to Denmark. Thereafter Sveinn went east to Garðar[82] and never returned.

XXV. Later Óláfr asked for the hand of Ástríðr, the daughter of Óláfr sœnski and the sister of Ingigerðr, to whom he

hennar heitum þeim fyr reiði sakar, ok gifti Jaritláfi Austrvegs konungi, ok gat Óláfr digri með henni bǫrn. En þeira ørnefni eða ørferðir vitum vér eigi, nema um Gunnhildi dóttur þeira, er tók Ottó hertogi á Saxlandi. Óláfr var fríðr sýnum ok listuligr, jarpt[a] [o] hár hafði hann ok rauðara skegg, riðvaxinn[b] meðalmaðr, [oo][c] ekki hǫ́r. Hann var á .xx.[d] aldri er hann kom í Nóreg, ok sýndisk vitrum mǫnnum í Nóregi hann mikit afbragð í vizku sinni, ok ǫllum vaskleik um hvern mann fram.

XXVI. ⟨E⟩n á þessu méli réð Knútr fyr Englandi, er hann hafði unnit með hjǫlp ok með fulltingi ens helga Óláfs, ok launaði inum helga Óláfi eigi betr en hann bar fé undir hǫfðingja er í Nóregi vǫru—sem síðan reyndisk—at þeir skyldu svíkja landit undan hónum. Var í þeiri tǫlu Erlingr á Sóla, Kálfr á Eggju, Þórir hundr ok margir aðrir. En þá er inn helgi Óláfr fór austr til móts við Knút konung, þá mœtti hann Erlingi ok vænti at hann væri[e] til liðveizlu kominn í mót[f] hónum. En hann réð til konungs þá með bardaga, ok helt orrostu við hann, ok vann inn helgi Óláfr sigr, ok varð Erlingr svá nauðstaddr at engi var annarr kostr en hann hljóp á miskunn konungs, ok hann veitti hónum vǫrn þá er aðrir sóttu at hónum. En Áslákr hét maðr Fitjaskalli, er stafnbúi var konungs. Hann gekk aftr á skip ok hafði undir skauti sér leyniliga handøxi, ok varð engi fyrr varr við en hann hafði hǫggvit hann í hǫfuð banasár, ok kvað svá at orði: 'Svá skal marka níðinginn!' En konungrinn svaraði: 'Nú hefir þú hǫggvit Nóreg ór hendi mér.' En þá varð hann varr af þeim mǫnnum er þar tók hann at allir stœrstu menn í landinu vǫru í svikum við

[a] MS apparently jarpr, suggesting an original jarpr á hár.
[b] hafði . . . riðvaxinn] these words are written over an erasure.
[c] probably en.
[d] written in the margin in the same hand is [a] tvitv[gs] aldri.
[e] written vari, probably simply an error.
[f] -veizlu . . . mót] the word náliga is written in the margin next to this line, apparently

had previously been betrothed. Her father had broken off that betrothal out of anger and had given her to Yaroslav, king of Russia.[83] Óláfr digri had some children by Ástríðr, but with the exception of their daughter Gunnhildr, whom Duke Otto of Saxony married, their names and fates are unknown.[84]

Óláfr was handsome and good-looking, with reddish-brown hair and a redder beard, squarely built and of medium height, not tall. He was in his twentieth year when he came to Norway, and to wise men in Norway he seemed outstanding in his wisdom and in all valour surpassing other men.

XXVI. At this time Knútr ruled England, which he had won with the help and support of St Óláfr,[85] but he rewarded him no better than by bribing the chieftains who were in Norway into betraying the country away from him, as later happened. Among these chieftains were Erlingr of Sóli, Kálfr of Egg, Þórir hundr and many others. And when St Óláfr went east against King Knútr he met Erlingr, whom he supposed to be there to support him, but Erlingr turned against him and fought him in battle.[86] St Óláfr won the victory and Erlingr was in such straits that there was no alternative but to go and put himself at the king's mercy, and the king protected him when others attacked him. But a man named Áslákr Fitjaskalli,[87] the king's forecastleman, walked to the stern of the ship with a hand-axe concealed under his cloak, and before anyone had noticed, he struck Erlingr a mortal wound on the head and spoke these words: 'Thus shall the nithing[88] be branded.' The king answered: 'Now you have struck Norway from my hand.' And from the men he captured there, the king learned that all the most important men in the country were involved in his

in the same hand. It does not, however, appear to fit into this or any of the surrounding sentences.

hann. Ok snørisk hann þá norðr í fjǫrð þann er heitir Sleygsarfjǫrðr, inn frá Borgund,[a] ok gekk þar af skipum ok upp at dal þeim er heitir Valdalr, ok helt síðan ór landi á fjǫgrtánda vetri síz hann kom í land,[b] ok því næst í Austrvega, ok hafði sun sinn með sér, Magnús góða.

XXVII. ⟨E⟩n Knútr skipar þá í ríki fyrst Hǫkoni systursyni sínum, ok gíslaði land undir sik af allra baztra manna sunum, en lagði fólkið til áþjánar ok til hlýðskyldis.[c] En Hǫkon fórsk um várit eftir í Englandshafi, en er Knútr frá þat, þá setti hann Svein, sun sinn, ok Álfífu móður hans í ríkit.

XXVIII. ⟨V⟩ar þá í fyrstu svá mikit danskra manna metorð at eins þeira vitni skyldi rinda tíu Norðmanna.[d] Engi skyldi ná af landi at fara nema með konungs leyfi, en ef fœri þá felli undir konung eignir þess. En hverr er mann vægi skyldi hafa fyrvegit landi ok lausum eyri. Ef maðr varð í útlegð ok tœmðisk hónum arfr, þá eignaðisk konungr arf þann.

XXIX. ⟨A⟩t jólum skyldi hverr búandi konungi fá af arni hverjum mæli malts ok lær af oxa þrévetrum—þat var kallat vinar[e] toddi—ok spann smjǫrs, ok húsfreyja hver rykkjartó—þat var lín órengt[f] svá mikit at spennt fengi umb mesta fingri ok lengsta. Búendr skyldir[g] ok at gera hús þau ǫll er konungr vildi hafa á bústǫðum sínum. Sjǫ menn skyldu[h] gera einn liðfœran, ok gera fyrir hvern er .v. vetra gamall væri, ok þar eftir hǫmlur eiga. Hverr maðr er

---

[a] *MS* borgung.

[b] á . . . land] *added in the margin in the same hand.*

[c] *the first element of this word is normally* lýð- (*from* lýðr, '*people*'), *but is written with an* h *both here and on the next page, probably due to folk-etymology relating it to* hlýða, '*obey*'.

[d] *first written thus and then changed, incorrectly, to* norþmenn.

[e] *this should probably read* vinjar; *see Seip 1955, 163; Noreen 1923, § 383.*

[f] *this should perhaps be read* órennt; *cf.* áeggjan *and* Eggjar-Kálfr, *both written with* -eng- (*notes e on p. 4 and a on p. 42*).

betrayal. He turned north into the fjord called Sleygsarfjǫrðr, in from Borgund, and there he left his ships and went up the valley called Valdalr and thereafter he left the country, in the fourteenth winter after his arrival in the country, and went to Russia and he took with him his son, Magnús góði.

XXVII. Knútr first set his nephew Hákon over the kingdom and secured the country by taking hostage the sons of the most important men, and he oppressed the people and made them do him homage. But Hákon drowned the following spring in the North Sea and when Knútr received word of this he set his son Sveinn and Ælfgyfu, Sveinn's mother, over the kingdom.[89]

XXVIII. There was in the beginning such high regard for Danish men that the testimony of one of them would overturn that of ten Norwegians. No one could leave the country without the king's permission, but if anyone did leave, his possessions were forfeit to the king. And whosoever killed a man would lose land and chattels, and if a man were in outlawry and succeeded to inheritance, that inheritance was the king's.

XXIX. At Yule each farmer was to give the king a measure of malt for each hearth, a ham from a three-year-old ox—this was called 'a bit of the meadow'[90]—and a measure of butter; and each housewife should supply a 'lady's tow'[91]— that was as much clean flax as could be clasped between thumb and middle finger. The farmers were also to build all the houses the king wished to have on his estates. Each seven men were to outfit one able-bodied man—and this included all who had reached the age of five—who would thereafter man an oar.[92] Each man who went fishing was

---

[g] *i. e.* vǫru skyldir.
[h] *thus MS; some editors, e. g. Finnur Jónsson (Ágrip 1929, 30), have emended to* skyldi.

á haf røri skyld⟨i⟩ gjalda konungi landvǫrðu hvaðan sem hann røri, en þat eru fimm fiskar. Skip hvert er føri af landi braut skyldi konungr hlaða rúm yfir þvert skip. Maðr hverr er til Íslands føri skyldi gjalda landaura, hérlenzkr ok útlenzkr. Ok helzk sjá hlýðskyldi til þess er Sigurðr konungr Jórsalafari gaf af ok brøðr hans flestar þessar ánauðir.

XXX. ⟨E⟩n þó at sjá nauð ok illing lægi á landi, þá treystusk menn eigi uppreist at veita fyrir suna sinna sakar er í gísling vǫru.

XXXI. ⟨E⟩n eftir þetta þá sœkir inn helgi Óláfr aftr í land um Svíþjóð, ok kom af Jamtalandi til Þróndheims, ok kom niðr í Veradali, ok tók þá Eggjar-Kálfr[a] uppreist á mót hónum ok efldi orrostu með ǫllu megni, bæði fyrir kapps sakar ok illsku, ok fekk með sér fjǫlmenni, allra helzt fyr þess sakar at kristniboð hans kœmi eigi á landit, er menn vissu at hann myndi ný bjóða[b] ok styrkja með ǫllu megni, sem fyrr hafði hann gert, ok fekk þó þat til orðs at góðra manna synir skyldu eigi fyrir gísl [oooo][c] vera, ok helt orrostu við Óláf konung á Stiklastǫðum. Þeir vǫru hǫfðingjar fyr liði Þrœnda með Kálfi: Þórir hundr, Erlendr ór Gerði, Áslákr af Finneyjum. En með Óláfi vǫru í ferð Haraldr bróðir hans, .xv. vetra gamall, enn vænsti maðr ok mikill vexti,[d] Rǫgnvaldr Brúsasunr, ok Bjǫrn enn digri. Í þeiri orrostu fell Erlendr ór Gerði fyrstr manna ór Þrœnda liði. Þat var ok snemma orrostu er Óláfr konungr fell. Hann hafði sverð í hendi, en hvárki hafði hann hjálm né brynju. Hann fekk [oo] sár af húskarli Kálfs á kné. Þá hneig hann [oooooo] ok bazk fyrir ok skaut niðr sverðinu. Þórir hundr

[a] *written* engiar calfr.
[b] ný bjóða] *the preposition* á *may be missing before* ný, *or this could be a compound verb, otherwise unattested*; ný *could conceivably also be the adjective* (*with* kristniboð).
[c] *here four letters have been partially erased*; *Storm believed them to have been* slom (*the* sl *would be in that case a dittography*), *but Dahlerup* (*Ágrip 1880, 113*) *is*

to pay the king a 'land bundle' from wherever he put out, and this was five fish. On each ship sailing from the country the king was to load a space across the ship. Each man who sailed to Iceland, native or foreign,[93] was to pay a land tax. These obligations remained until Sigurðr Jórsalafari and his brothers abolished most of these impositions.[94]

XXX. And even though such evil and oppression lay on the country, men dared not rise up for the sake of their sons who were held hostage.

XXXI. Later St Óláfr returned to Norway through Sweden and came from Jamtaland to Þrándheimr and came down in Veradalr, and then Kálfr of Egg, because of his malevolence and eagerness to fight, rose against him and prepared for battle with all his might. He gained the support of many men, mostly those who wished to keep Óláfr's Christian preaching from the country, for they knew that he would again preach it and support it with all his power as he had done before. But Kálfr gave as his pretext that the sons of good men should not be held hostage and fought King Óláfr in battle at Stiklastaðir.[95]

These were the chieftains leading the Þrœndir's army with Kálfr: Þórir hundr, Erlendr of Gerði, Áslákr of Finneyjar. On Óláfr's side were his brother Haraldr, fifteen years of age, a handsome man of great stature, Rǫgnvaldr Brúsason and Bjǫrn digri.[96]

In that battle Erlendr of Gerði fell first of the Þrœndir's army. It was also early in the battle that King Óláfr fell. He had a sword in his hand, but had neither helmet nor mailcoat. He was wounded in the knee by one of Kálfr's men. He sank down and prayed and threw down his sword. Þórir

unconvinced. The first two letters appear to have ascenders and could therefore be sl; *they could, however, also be* fl, ft *or* st, *and the third and fourth letters look more like* vr *than* om. *None of these combinations produces anything that fits the context, however.*

[d] enn . . . vexti] *written over an erasure.*

ok Þorsteinn knarrasmiðr báru banorð af Óláfi konungi. Ok steig svá enn helgi Óláfr af þeiri orrostu ór þessu ríki í himinríki. Bjǫrn enn digri fell at hǫfði konunginum, en Þorsteinn knarrasmiðr var þegar drepinn á fœtr konunginum. Í þeiri orrostu fell Áslákr af Finneyjum, ok fjǫlði manna af Þrœnda liði.

XXXII. ⟨E⟩n þá tók landsfólkit eftir fall konungs fulliga við vesǫld þangat út er Sveinn var ok Álfífa. Ok var þá hǫrmuligt undir því ríki at búa, bæði með ófrelsi ok með óárani, er fólkit lifði meir við búfjár mat en manna, fyr því at aldregi var ár á þeira dǫgum, sem heyra má í vísu þessi er Sigvatr kvað:

3. Álfífu mon ævi
   ungr drengr muna lengi
   er oxa mat ǫ́tu
   inni skaf sem hafrar;
   annat var, þá er Óláfr
   ógnbandaðr réð landi,
   hverr átti þá hrósa[a]
   hjalmar hlǫðnu[b] korni.

XXXIII. ⟨E⟩n inn helgi Óláfr bar þessa heims .xv. vetr konungs nafn í Nóregi til þess er hann fell. Þá var hann hálffertøgr at aldri, ok var þá er hann fell frá burð dróttins várs þúshundrað vetra ok .ix. vetr ok .xx. En í orrostu þeiri er inn helgi Óláfr fell í, þá varð Haraldr bróðir hans sárr. Hann flýði eftir fall hans braut ýr landi ok[c] í Austrvega ok svá til Miklagarðs, ok segja sumir at hann tœki konungs nafn í Nóregi,[d] en sumir synja.

[a] *following this word there is a space, large enough for about eight letters, which seems to have been left blank by the scribe.*

[b] hjalmar hlǫðnu] *most editors see this as a corruption of* hjálmþornuðu.

[c] braut . . . ok] *written over an erasure. There is a full stop after* hans, *which suggests that the next word was either* ok *or* en.

[d] í Nóregi] *added above the line.*

hundr and Þorsteinn knarrasmiðr dealt King Óláfr his death blow. And thus in that battle St Óláfr rose from this kingdom to the kingdom of heaven. Bjǫrn digri fell before the king and Þorsteinn knarrasmiðr was killed right on the king's heels. In this battle Áslákr of Finneyjar fell and many men of the Þrœndir's army.

XXXII. After the death of the king, the people's misery became complete under Sveinn and Ælfgyfu. It was miserable living under their rule, both because of their tyranny and the bad seasons, when the people lived more off cattle fodder than the food of men, because the seasons were never good in their time, as can be heard from this verse by Sighvatr:[97]

> 3. Ælfgyfu's time
> long will the young man remember,
> when they at home ate ox's food,
> and like the goats, ate rind;
> different it was when Óláfr,
> the warrior, ruled the land,
> then everyone could enjoy
> stacks of dry corn.

XXXIII. St Óláfr had borne in this world the name of king in Norway for fifteen years when he fell. He was then thirty-five years of age and it was, when he fell, one thousand and twenty-nine winters from the birth of Our Lord.[98] In the battle in which St Óláfr fell his brother Haraldr was wounded, and after Óláfr's death he fled the country to Russia and went thereafter to Mikligarðr, and some say that he claimed the kingly title in Norway, but others deny this.[99]

XXXIV. ⟨E⟩n þá er guð tók at birta jartegnum um inn helga Óláf, þá réðusk ⟨inir⟩ bǫztu menn til at fara ór landi at sœkja Magnús, sun ins helga Óláfs, þvíat menn fundu misræði sín ok iðruðusk, ok vildu þá þat bœta á syni hans er þeir hǫfðu á sjǫlfum hónum brotit, ok sóttu í Austrvega til Jaritláfs konungs, ok bǫru til þess allra baztra manna orðsending ok bœnarstað at hann skyldi til lands sœkja. Ok vǫru hǫfðing⟨j⟩ar í þeiri fǫr Rǫgnvaldr jarl, Einarr þambaskelmir, Sveinn bryggjufót⟨r⟩, Kálfr Árnasunr. En þeira bœn var eigi fyrr heyrð né framgeng en þeir unnu hónum land ok trúnað, þvíat Ingigerðr dróttning stóð á móti.

XXXV. ⟨E⟩n því næst kømr hann í land fjórum vetrum eftir fall fǫður síns Óláfs konungs, ok með því at þau Sveinn ok Álfífa vissu manna þokka við hann ok óvinsælð sína, þá flýðu þau til Danmarkar. En Magnús konungr tók við ríki með alþýðu þokka of síðir, þóat með margs angri væri fyrst, þvíat hann hóf ríki sitt með harðræði fyr œsku sinnar sakar[a] ok ágirndar rǫðuneytis. Hann var náliga .xi. vetra er hann kom í land. Hann átti þing í Niðarósi, ok reisti með freku sakargift við Þrœndi alla, ok stungu allir nefi í skinnfeld ok veittu allir þǫgn, en engi andsvǫr. Stóð upp þá maðr, Atli at nafni, ok mælti eigi fleiri orð en þessur: 'Svá skorpnar skór at fœti mér at ek má eigi ór stað komask.' En Sigvatr kvað þar þegar vísu þessa:

> 4. Hætt er þat er allir ætla,
> áðr skal við því ráða,
> hárir menn er ek heyri,
> hót, skjǫldungi á móti.
> Gneyft[b] er þat, er hǫfðum hnifta[c]
> heldr ok niðr í feldi,

---

[a] sinnar sakar] MS sacar sinar, *but with superscript letters to indicate inversion.*
[b] gneyft] *frequently emended to* greypt.
[c] hnifta] MS hniftir; *frequently emended to* hneppta.

XXXIV. When God began to provide miraculous proof of St Óláfr,[100] the most important men decided to go abroad and fetch Magnús, St Óláfr's son, for men had realised their mistake and had repented and wished to make up to Óláfr's son the offence that they had caused Óláfr himself to suffer. They went to Russia to King Yaroslav, bearing the message of all the most important men and their request that he return to Norway. The leading men on this expedition were Jarl Rǫgnvaldr, Einarr þambarskelmir, Sveinn bryggjufótr and Kálfr Árnason. But their request was neither heard nor granted until they had pledged Magnús both the country and their loyalty, because Queen Ingigerðr was opposed.

XXXV. He returned to Norway four years after the death of his father King Óláfr, and Sveinn and Ælfgyfu, knowing of his favour with the people and of their own unpopularity, fled to Denmark. And Magnús took the kingdom with the good will of the people in the end, though in the beginning he was the cause of many grievances, for because of his youth and the ambition of his advisers he began his rule harshly.[101] He was nearly eleven years old when he came to the country.

He held assembly in Niðaróss and began by acrimoniously making accusations against all the Prœndir, and they all stuck their noses in their cloaks, and were silent and gave no answer. Then a man named Atli stood up and said no more words than these: 'So shrinks the shoe on my foot that I cannot move.'

Sighvatr spoke this verse then and there:

> 4. Dangerous is the threat
>   —this must first be dealt with—
>   when all the elders, as I hear,
>   would rise against their king.
>   It is dangerous too
>   when the assembled men bow their heads

slegit hefir þǫgn á þegna,
þingmenn nǫsum stinga.

Ok raufsk þing þat með ⟨þeima⟩ hætti at konungr bað alla menn finnask þar um morgininn. Ok fannsk þá í hans orðum at guð hafði skipt skapi hans, ok var þá freka snúin til miskunnar. Hét ǫllum mǫnnum gœzku ok efndi sem hann hét, eða betr, ok aflaðisk hónum af því vinsæl⟨d⟩ mikil, ok nafn þat at hann var kallaðr Mǫgnús góði.

XXXVI. ⟨E⟩n þá er hann hafði nǫkkvura vetr landi stýrt, lǫgum skipat, ok ǫllum góðum siðum ok kristni styrkt, þá minntisk hann á rǫngyndi þau er við fǫður hans hǫfðu verit gǫr, ok helt her til Danmarkar, er allir vǫru fullfúsir fyrir hefnda sakar. En þá var Sveinn frá fallinn í Danmǫrku ok svá Knútr faðir hans í Englandi, ok réð þá fyrir Danmǫrku bróðir Sveins, Hǫrða-Knútr at nafni,[a] ok helt her á móti Magnúsi ok fundusk í Brenneyjum. Fóru vitrir menn á meðal ok mæltu til sættar, ok gerðu með þeima hætti at með því at Knúti þótti sem hann ætti rétt tilmæli til Nóregs, þá hafði faðir hans aflat ok bróðir hans at setit—Mǫgnúsi þótti ok illt misheldi þat er faðir hans hafði haft af Knúti, svik[b] ok lands flótta ok lífs aftak—þá slǿru þeir þó máli í þá sætt at sá þeira er lengr lifði skyldi taka við bǿðum landum, ok hvárr sínu ríki ráða meðan báðir lifði þeir, ok settu gísla, ok andaðisk Knútr fyrri, en Mǫgnús tók þá við Danmǫrk fyr útan gagnmæli, þvíat synir bǿztu manna vǫru í gíslinginni.

XXXVII. ⟨E⟩n þá er Sveinn, sunr Úlfs ok Ástríðar, systur Knúts ríkja, spurði þetta í England, þá aflaði hann alla vega hers er hann mátti. En Mǫgnús ⟨fór⟩ at móti ok funnusk á skipum við nes þat er kallat er Helganes ok

---

[a] written nāfNi (cf. note b, p. 8 above).
[b] MS svit.

and stick their noses in their cloaks;
the thanes are struck silent.[102]

And the assembly broke up with the king's request that all meet there the following morning. And then it could be heard from his words that God had changed his disposition and his acrimony was turned then to mercy. He promised all men kindness and kept what he had promised, or better, and as a result gained great popularity and the name by which he was called: Magnús góði.

XXXVI. After he had ruled the country for several years, established laws and good customs and strengthened Christianity, he remembered the injustices that had been done his father and went with an army to Denmark. They were all eager to go for the sake of revenge.

But in Denmark Sveinn had died and so had his father Knútr in England, and Denmark was then ruled by Sveinn's brother, who was called Hǫrða-Knútr,[103] and he led an army against Magnús and they met at Brenneyjar. Wise men acted as intermediaries and an agreement was proposed and made in such a way that since Hǫrða-Knútr thought that he had rightful claim to Norway because his father had won it and his brother had ruled it—and Magnús thought too that his father had suffered great wrong at the hands of Knútr, betrayal, exile, death—this agreement was reached: the one who lived the longer was to rule both countries, but each would rule his own kingdom while both lived.[104] Then hostages were exchanged. Knútr died first,[105] and Magnús then took Denmark without opposition, because the sons of the most important men were held hostage.

XXXVII. When Sveinn, son of Úlfr and Knútr ríki's sister Ástríðr,[106] heard news of this in England, he gathered forces together from wherever he could. Magnús came against him and they met with their ships off the peninsula

heldu bardaga, ok flýði Sveinn til Vinnlands ok efldi þaðan her annat sinni, hvaðan ok er hann mátti fá, ok helt þeim her til Danmarkar, svát Mǫgnús hafði skǫmmu áðr vitorð af, ok fyrir því lítinn viðbúnað, ok óttaðisk af liðleysi, ok bjósk þó sem hann mátti til viðrtǫku.

XXXVIII. ⟨E⟩n of nóttina er hann skyldi berjask of morguninn, ok hónum var ótti mikill á ráði sínu, þá birtisk hónum faðir hans í draumi, ok bað hann ekki óttask, sagði hónum at hann skyldi sigr vinna, ok svá gafsk. Mœttusk þeir um morguninn á heiði þeiri er Hlýrskógsheiðr heitir, er liggr við Skotborgarǫ́, ok skipaði Mǫgnús svá liði sínu í fylkingar, sem inn helgi Óláfr hafði áðr í draumi kennt hónum, ok á þeiri tíð gekk hann at berjask er hann hafði áðr sagt hónum of nóttina. Þat var þá er sól var í landsuðri, ok kom fylking hans á arm fylkingu Sveins, ok snørisk hón ǫll fyrir, ok fekk Sveinn af mǫrgu því mikinn skaða er hann hafði áðr til sigrs ætlat, þvíat hann hafði øxnum[a] skipat í odd á liði sínu, ok bundit spjót á bak, en fjalar fyr augu. En nautin snørusk fyrst á frá, ok veik svá til at Sveinn var netjaðr meðal nautaflokksins ok flokks Mǫgnúss, ok fekk inn mesta Sveinn[b] mannskaða, en hann freltisk[c] með flótta, ok rak Mǫgnús lengi með annan mann Svein ok flokk hans. En þat var orðlag Sveins sagt ok hans manna at ef allir berðisk svá sem sá enn fríði maðr enn ungi í silkiskyrtunni, þá hefði ekki barn undan komizk, en þat var konungrinn sjálfr, ok vendi aftr síðan til hers síns, ok urðu allir hónum fegnir. En áðr hǫfðu þeir óttazk fall hans, er hann dvalðisk svá lengi at reka flokkinn með eins manns hjǫlp. En Sveinn sótti sér friðland. Mǫgnús konungr sitr nú í Danmǫrku með kyrrð ok með fullum friði.

---

[a] written voxnom; *presumably an error.*
[b] inn mesta Sveinn] *the word-order* Sveinn inn mesta *would be more natural.*
[c] *i. e.* frelstisk (*cf. p. 66, three lines up*).

called Helganes and there fought.[107] Sveinn fled to Wendland and there gathered an army a second time, also from wherever he could. He brought this army to Denmark in such a way that Magnús remained unaware of his coming until shortly beforehand and had therefore made little preparation and was afraid that his men would be too few. He nevertheless prepared as best he could for defence.

XXXVIII. During the night before the morning he was to fight, as he was greatly apprehensive about his situation, his father appeared to him in a dream and told him not to fear and told him that he would gain victory, and so it came to pass.

They met that morning on the heath called Hlýrskógsheiðr, which lies near Skotborgará,[108] and Magnús arrayed his forces in detachments as St Óláfr had instructed him in the dream and went into battle at the time Óláfr had told him to during the night. That was when the sun was in the southeast, and his forces came upon one wing of Sveinn's army, who all turned, and Sveinn was harmed greatly by many of the things that he had intended to bring him victory, because he had had oxen placed at the front of his ranks, with spears tied to their backs and wooden boards before their eyes, but the cattle turned back and so it happened that Sveinn was trapped between the herd of cattle and Magnús's troops. Sveinn suffered the greater losses and escaped through flight, and Magnús and one other man pursued Sveinn and his forces for a long time. Sveinn and his men said that if all had fought as had the handsome young man in the silken shirt, then not a child would have got away—and that man was the king himself. Magnús then turned back to his men and all were relieved to see him. Earlier they had feared that he had been killed, when he had been so long in pursuing Sveinn's army with the help of only one man. Sveinn sought asylum. King Magnús now ruled Denmark in peace and complete tranquillity.

XXXIX. ⟨E⟩n nú er á stundina líðr, þá sœkir Haraldr, bróðir ens helga Óláfs, heim ór Garði um Austrveg á kaupskipi, vel búinn at fé ok at gørsimum, ok lendi at í Danmǫrk, þar er konungrinn Mǫgnús vissi hvárki til hans né til skips hans, ok háttar svá at hann kom þar í nǿnd sem konungrinn var, ok kom þeim ráðgjafa konungs Mǫgnúss á fund[a] við sik er Úlfr hét stalleri, ok talaði við hann mál Haralds sem hann væri sendimaðr Haralds, en eigi sjálfr Haraldr. Bað hann síðan at Úlfr skyldi frétta konunginn Mǫgnús hvessu hann myndi taka við fǫðurbrœðr sínum ef hann sœtti í land aftr; kvað verðleika mikinn á vera at vel væri við hónum tekit. 'Tel ek til þess,' kvað hann, 'skyldu þeira ok fylgð þá er hann hafði veitt enum helga Óláfi, brœðr sínum ok fǫður Mǫgnúss,' kvað ok Harald vera vizkan[b] mann ok styrkjan, ok mǫrg ok mikil stórvirki hafa drýgt útan lands, maðr ok nú vel at fé búinn ok at gersimum, ok af ǫllu þessu mega hann mikinn styrk veita frænda sínum, ok mega standa ok til mikils vanda ef hans viðrtaka væri eigi með veg. En Úlfr tók glaðliga við þessu ørendi. Konungrinn Mǫgnús tók ok glaðliga undir, kvað sik af ǫllum góðum drengjum er hann hafði með sér vætta mikils styr⟨k⟩s ok góðs rǿðuneytis, en myklu mest þar sem fǫðurbróðir hans var. En eftir þessur ansvǫr konungs sœkir Haraldr til skips, en því næst á fund frænda síns, ok kenndi Úlfr þann enn mikla mann ok inn listuliga þá vera Harald er áðr hafði kallaz⟨k⟩ sendimaðr Haralds. Var hér nú síðan mikill fagnaðarfundr frænda, ok tekr Haraldr við hólfum Nóregi, ok til sœkir sem bæði leiddi hann til ætterni ok svá góð gjǫf góðs konungs, þvíat Haraldr var sunr Sigurðar sýrar, en Sigurðr sunr Hálfdanar—er sumir kǫlluðu heikilnef, en sumir hvítbein— en Hálfdan sunr Sygurðar[c] hrísa, er var sunr Haralds hárfagra.

[a] *first written* fundi, *but* i *erased.*
[b] *apparently first written* uitran, *but 'corrected' by changing* r *to* þ *and adding* c *above the line* (uitþcan).
[c] *written* sugurþar; Syg- *for* Sig- *in personal names was particularly common in Norway (cf. Noreen 1923, § 77.5 a Anm. 3).*

XXXIX. But as time went on, Haraldr, brother of St Óláfr, returned home from Mikligarðr through Russia on a merchant ship, well provided with treasure and goods,[109] and he landed in Denmark at a place where King Magnús knew nothing of him or of his ship. And so it happened that he came near to where the king was and got one of King Magnús's advisers, whose name was Úlfr stalleri,[110] to meet with him, and he discussed with him Haraldr's situation, as though he were Haraldr's messenger rather than Haraldr himself. He then asked Úlfr to enquire as to how King Magnús might receive his father's brother if he were to return to the country and said that he very much deserved to be well received. 'The reason for this,' he said, 'as I see it, is that they are kinsmen and because of the support he gave St Óláfr, his brother and Magnús's father.' He also said Haraldr was a wise and powerful man who had done many great deeds abroad, a man now also well provided with money and treasure, and through this he could give his nephew much support. But if he were not received with honour, great ill could come of it.

Úlfr undertook this errand gladly and King Magnús responded favourably and said that he expected much support and good counsel from all the good men he had with him, but especially from his uncle.

After the king's answer, Haraldr returned to his ship and proceeded then to meet his nephew. Then Úlfr realised that the great and handsome man who had earlier called himself Haraldr's messenger was Haraldr himself. It was then a very joyful meeting for the kinsmen,[111] and Haraldr accepted half of Norway and took it as he had right to, both by descent and because of the good king's good gift, because Haraldr was the son of Sigurðr sýr and Sigurðr son of Hálfdan, whom some called heikilnef[112] and others hvítbeinn, and Hálfdan the son of Sigurðr hrísi, who was the son of Haraldr hárfagri.

XL. ⟨E⟩n Mǫgnús réð síðan Danmǫrk ok hǫlfum Nóregi með kyrrð ok með[a] ró fyrir útan allt ákall meðan hann lifði, ok réð alls hvǫrutveggja ríkinu .xiij. vetr með þeim sex er hann hafði Danmǫrk, ok fekk sótt á Sjólandi ok andaðisk þar vetri síðarr en Haraldr kœmi í land, fǫðurbróðir hans. Þá hafði hann náliga .iiij. vetr ok .xx.[b] En lík hans var fœrt norðr í Þróndheim ok nið⟨r⟩ sett[c] í Kristskirkju, þar sem faðir hans hvílir. Ok var þetta h⟨v⟩ǫrutveggja landinu mikill harmdauði, þvíat engi lifði afspringr eftir hann nema ein dóttir, er hann fell í frá á ungum aldri. En í sótt sinni gerði hann Þóri, bróður sinn sammœðra, til Sveins Úlfssunar með þeim hætti at hann sagði hónum eigi andlát hans, sagði heldr svá at hann hafði hónum gefit upp ríkit. En Sveinn þóttisk þó vita andlát hans ok tók með blíðu við mikilli gjǫf ok sótti til ok lét standa alla þá skipan er hann hafði skipat í ríkinu, ok svá gjafar bæði við Þóri bróður hans ok svá við alla aðra.

XLI. ⟨E⟩n Haraldr konungr tekr[d] nú einn við[e] ǫllum Nóregi ok stýrði með herðu mikilli ok þó með góðum friði, ok var eigi sá annarr konungr er ǫllum mǫnnum stœði agi jammikill af fyr vizku sakir ok [oooooo] atgervi. En Haraldr kvángaðisk brátt er hann kom í land, ok tók bróðurdóttur manns þess er Fiðr hét, er bjó austr á Ranríki, kynstórr maðr ok at auð vel búinn, ok veitti hann mági sínum, Haraldr konungr,[f] veizlur miklar, ok gerðisk svá til enn síðan at hann vildi þær rjúfa, ok gerðisk af því misdeild með þeim, ok sótti Fiðr[g] ór landi með frændagengi sitt, ok sótti til Sveins konungs í Danmǫrku með .xij. langskipum ok þá af hónum jarls nafn, vísaði heim þeim sem fylgt hǫfðu hónum, vildi

---

[a] added above the line.
[b] following this the words at aldri have been partially erased and En written in the space.
[c] niðr sett] written niþ setr, but with the r partially erased, suggesting the scribe may simply have put it in the wrong place (cf. p. 64, line 5); alternatively, nið might be a variant form.
[d] following this is written einn, partially erased.
[e] MS uil. [f] Haraldr konungr] MS haraldi konungi.
[g] reading uncertain; either fiþ or fiþ̃, i. e. síðan, or, more likely, síðar.

XL. Thereafter Magnús ruled Denmark and half of Norway in peace and tranquillity without further claims for as long as he lived. He ruled both kingdoms thirteen winters in all, including the six he ruled Denmark, and he fell ill in Sjóland and died there a year after his uncle Haraldr's return.[113] He was then nearly twenty-four years old. His body was moved north to Þrándheimr and buried in Kristskirkja, where his father rests.[114] His death was much lamented in both countries, for no offspring survived him but for one daughter,[115] dying as he did at this early age.

But while he had lain ill, he had sent his half-brother Þórir to Sveinn Úlfsson; Þórir was not to tell Sveinn that King Magnús had died, but rather that he had given him the kingdom. But Sveinn realised that Magnús had died and accepted the great gift joyfully. He took the kingdom and allowed to stand all the arrangements Magnús had made in the kingdom, and also the gifts to his brother Þórir and to everyone else.

XLI. King Haraldr now took sole rule over all Norway and ruled with great severity, yet peacefully. There was not another king who, because of his wisdom and his accomplishments, inspired as much awe in all his people.

Soon after coming to Norway, Haraldr married the niece of a man named Finnr, a man of good family and great wealth who lived to the east in Ranríki.[116] King Haraldr granted his wife's uncle great revenues, but later it happened that he wished to put a stop to these and they quarrelled as a result.[117] Finnr thereafter left the country with his kinsfolk and went to King Sveinn in Denmark with seven longships and received from him the title of jarl. He sent home those who had accompanied him, for he did not wish that they should lose their property or their wives or children. He and Sveinn gathered together forces

eigi at þeir léti eignir sínar, svági konur eða bǫrn. En Sveinn ok hann drógu sveit saman ok fóru með her í Nóreg, ok Haraldr konungr at móti, ok mœttusk við Nizi í Danmǫrk á Hallandi, ok lá Haraldr við ey þá er inn er við meginland, ok hugðusk þeir Sveinn at sitja hónum vatn, þvíat eigi vissu menn vatn í eynni. En Haraldr konungr lét leita ef ormr kvikr fyndisk í eynni, ok hann fannsk ok var mœddr síðan við eld at ráði konungs, at hann skyldi þyrsta sem mest. Var síðan þrǿðr bundinn við sporðinn ok hann lauss látinn. Sótti hann þegar til vats at drekka ok var svá vatn fundit. En þá er Haraldr þóttisk viðr búinn, þá lagði hann til bardaga þegar lið hans var komit, þat er hann lá á bið, ok var Sveinn sigraðr með miklu mannspelli, ok flýði undan með fámenni. En Fiðr varð hantekinn ok friðr gefinn, ok fluttisk heim með Haraldi til eigna sinna.

XLII. ⟨E⟩n þá er Haraldr hafði .xix. vetr ráðit fyrir Nóregi ǫllum síz Mǫgnús fell í frá, þá kømr maðr af Englandi, Tósti at nafni. Hann var jarl ok bróðir Haralds Goðinasonar, þess er þá réð fyr Englandi, ok jamborinn til lands við Harald, ok þó ǫllu sviptr, ok beiddisk liðveizlu af Haraldi ok hét hónum hǫlfu Englandi ef þeir fengi unnit. Ok Haraldr helt þangat her með hónum, ok unnu þeir allt Norðimbraland. En Englands konungr var þá í Normandie, ok þegar er hann spyrr, þá skundar hann aftr með her, ok kom þá svá á óvart at lið þeira var flest á skipum, en þeir vópnlausir náliga er uppi vǫru, fyr útan hǫggvópn ok hlífðarvópn. Þá snørusk þeir í eina fylking allir, ok bjoggusk við, en konungrinn sjálfr sat á hesti ok reið meðan hann fylkði liðinu, en hestrinn fell undir hónum ok varp hónum af baki. En konungrinn mælti er hann stóð upp: 'Sjaldan fór svá, þá er vel vildi,' kvað hann, ok svá var ok sem konungrinn

and went with an army to Norway. King Haraldr came against them and they met by the Niz in Halland in Denmark.[118] Haraldr lay by an island near to the mainland. Sveinn and Finnr thought to cut him off from fresh water, because no one thought there was water on the island. King Haraldr had men search for a live snake on the island. One was found and, following the king's direction, then exhausted by a fire so that it should get as thirsty as possible.[119] They then tied a string to its tail and set it free. It immediately sought drinking water and in this way water was found.

When Haraldr felt himself prepared and the men for whom he had been waiting arrived, he went into battle. Sveinn was defeated and suffered great losses and fled with a few men. But Finnr was captured and pardoned and returned home with Haraldr to his estates.

XLII. When Haraldr had ruled all Norway for nineteen years after the death of Magnús, a man came from England named Tostig.[120] He was a jarl and the brother of Harold Godwineson, who then ruled in England, and though his right of birth was equal to Harold's he was deprived of everything. He asked support of Haraldr and promised him half of England if they should win it. Haraldr took his army there with Tostig and they won all of Northumbria.

The king of England was then in Normandy, but as soon as he heard news of this he hurried back with an army and came so unexpectedly upon them that most of their troops were on board their ships, and those on land nearly unarmed but for striking weapons and weapons of defence. They all came together in one formation and made ready. Haraldr of Norway was on horseback and rode as he arrayed his troops. The horse stumbled and threw him off. The king said as he stood up: 'Seldom has it gone thus when fate was favourable.'[121] And it happened as the king

sagði, at hann varð eigi ljúgspár, fyrir því at í þeim bardaga enum sama of daginn fell[a] bæði Haraldr konungr ok Tósti jarl ok mikit lið með þeim, en þat flýði til skipa er undan kom. Var foringi fyrir liði því Óláfr, sunr Haralds, enn vænsti maðr,[b] náliga .xx., er búandi var kallaðr fyr spekðar sakar ok hógværis. En hann beiddisk [oooo][c] griða af Haraldi ok svá líkama fǫður síns, ok þá hvárt tveggja, fluttisk síðan [með Póli jarli][d] í Orkneyjar, en um várit eftir til Nóregs ok jarðaði [lík hans][e] í Máríukirkju í Niðarósi—en nú liggr hann á Elgjusetri—þvíat þat þótti fallit at hann fylgði kirkju þeiri er hann hafði látit gera, en Eysteinn erkibyskup lét þangat fara hreinlífismǫnnum undir hendr, ok aukaði með því þá eign aðra er hann sjálfr hafði þangat gefit.

XLIII. En þá .xij. mánaðr er Haraldr var vestr ok þeir feðgar, þá réð sunr hans fyrir Nóregi meðan, sá ⟨er⟩ Mǫgnús hét, enn fríðasti maðr, ok skipta þeir brœðr ok Óláfr nú ríki sín á miðal. En vǫnu skjótara,[f] .ij. vetrum síðarr, fell Mǫgnús á frá ok átti son eftir, þann er Hǫkon hét, ok var sá fenginn Steigar-Þóri til fóstrs. En Óláfr réð einn fyr Nóregi .iiij. vetr ok .xx. síðan, ok var um enkis konungs ævi eftir Harald hárfagra Nóregr í slíkri farsælu sem um hans daga, ok skipaði hann mǫrgum þeim mǫlum til vægðar er Haraldr hafði með freku reist ok haldit. Hann var mildr af gulli ok af silfri ok góðum gripum ok gersimum, en fastaldr[g] á jǫrðum. Olli vit hans því ok hitt, at hann sá at konungdóminum gegndi, ok eru mǫrg hans verk góð at inna.

---

[a] *following this word there is a space, large enough for four or five letters.*
[b] *something intended to follow this word is written in the margin; it cannot now be made out, but Storm was in his time able to read* er var at aldri (Ágrip *1880, 117*).
[c] *here four or five letters have been erased;* Dahlerup (Ágrip *1880, 117*) *suggests* oc fec.
[d] síðan . . . jarli] *there appears to have been an attempt made to erase these words.*

had said, and his prophecy was not false, for that day in that same battle both he and Jarl Tostig fell and many with them. Those who escaped fled to the ships. The leader of this group was Óláfr, Haraldr's son, a fine man, nearly twenty years old. He was called 'búandi' because he was quiet and gentle.[122] He asked quarter of Harold and also for the body of his father and was granted both. He then went to Orkney with Jarl Páll and the following spring to Norway. He buried Haraldr's body in Maríukirkja in Niðaróss—he now lies at Elgjusetr—because it was thought fitting that he remain with the church that he himself had had built. Archbishop Eysteinn had him moved there into the care of the monks and thus added to the other possessions he had himself given them.[123]

XLIII. The twelve months Haraldr and Óláfr were in the west, Haraldr's son, the one named Magnús, ruled Norway, a most handsome man, and he and his brother Óláfr now divided the kingdom between them. But, sooner than expected, two years later, Magnús died, leaving a son named Hákon, who was then fostered by Steigar-Þórir. Thereafter Óláfr ruled Norway alone for twenty-four years, and during no king's lifetime since Haraldr hárfagri had Norway seen such prosperity as in his day. He mitigated much which Haraldr harðráði had harshly begun and kept up. He was open-handed with gold and silver, valuables and treasures, but tight-fisted with land. The reason for this was his good sense and also that he saw that this would benefit his kingdom. And there are many of his good deeds to be related.

---

[e] lík hans] *added above the line; now all but unreadable.*

[f] *corrected by the scribe from* sciotare, *a Norwegianism (see Noreen 1923, § 442.1), which Seip (1955, 133) assumes derives from the exemplar.*

[g] *i. e.* fasthaldr.

XLIV. ⟨H⟩ann gerði upp steinkirkju at byskupsstólinum í Niðarósi yfir líkam ens helga Óláfs frænda síns, ok bjó hana til lykða. Ok hver hans gœzka hafi verið ok ástsemð við lýðinn, þá má skilja af orðum þeim er hann mælti dag nǫkkurn í Miklagildi. Var hann kátr ok í skapi góðu, ok gerðusk þeir til er þetta mæltu: 'Hérnú, fǫgnuðr er oss á, konungr, attu ert svá kátr.' En hann svaraði: 'Hví,' kvað hann, 'skal ek nú eigi vera kátr, er ek sé bæði á lýð mínum kæti ok frelsi, ok sit ek í samkundu þeiri er helguð er helgum fǫðurbróður mínum. Um daga fǫður míns þá var lýðr undir aga miklum ok ótta, ok fǫlu flestir menn gull sitt ok gersimar, en ek sé nú at á hverjum skínn er á, ok er þeira frelsi mín gleði.' Var ok svá gótt um hans daga at fyr útan orrostu þá friðaði hann fyrir sér ok fyrir lýð sínum útan lands, ok stóð hans næstu nágrǫnnum þó ógn af hónum, at hann væri hœgr ok hógværr, sem skáldit segr:[a]

5. Varði ógnar orðum
   Óláfr ok friðmǫlum
   jǫrð svá at engi þorði
   allvalda til kalla.

XLV. ⟨E⟩n þá er hann hafði ráðit Nóregi .vij. vetr ok .xx. með þeim enum fyrsta[b] er hann var vestr eftir fall Haralds, er Mǫgnús bróðir hans var í Nóregi, þá sýkðisk hann á bœ þeim er heitir Haukbœr, austr á Ranríki, þar sem hann tók veizlu, ok andaðisk þar, ok var líkamr hans fluttr norðr í Niðarós ok var jarðaðr[c] í kirkju þeiri er hann hafði látit gera.

XLVI.⟨E⟩n hér eftir stígr Mǫgnús berleggr,[d] sunr hans, til ríkis. Hann var þá náliga tvítugr er hann tók konungs nafn eftir fǫður sinn[e]—ok Hókon frændi hans annarr, er Steigar-Þórir hafði at fœða sem sagði fyrr; hann var vel hálfþrítøgr

---

[a] *apparently written* sego.   [b] MS frysta.
[c] *written* iarþar, *possibly only a slip, but on the loss of* /ð/ *before another consonant see Seip 1955, 157–60.*
[d] báin *or* béin, *i. e.* berbeinn, *is written above* Mǫgnús, *apparently in a younger hand.*
[e] Hann . . . sinn] *written over an erasure.*

XLIV. At the bishop's seat in Niðaróss he erected a stone church over the body of his uncle St Óláfr and saw to its completion.[124] And how great his kindness and love for his people were can be seen from the words he spoke one day at Miklagildi.[125] He was merry and in excellent humour, and some ventured to say: 'See now, it is pleasing to us, King, that you are so merry.' And he answered: 'Why should I not be merry when I see my people both happy and free, and I sit here at this feast in honour of my saintly uncle? In my father's day men lived in great awe and fear, and most hid their gold and treasures, but now I see that on every man shine his possessions. Their freedom is my joy.'

It was so good during his days that he made peace abroad without battle, both for himself and for his people. And even though he was quiet and gentle, his nearest neighbours stood in fear of him, as the poet says:

> 5. Through threatening words
> and peace-speeches
> Óláfr defended his country
> so that no king dared claim it.[126]

XLV. When he had ruled Norway for twenty-seven years, including the year he was in the west after the death of Haraldr and his brother Magnús was in Norway, he was taken ill at the farm called Haukbœr, eastward in Ranríki, where he was being feasted. He died there and his body was taken north to Niðaróss and there buried in the church he had had built.

XLVI. Thereafter his son Magnús berleggr took the kingdom.[127] He was nearly twenty when he took the kingly title after his father—along with his cousin Hákon, who had been fostered by Steigar-Þórir, as was said before; he

þá—ok vǫru einn vetr báðir ok þann í Niðarósi, ok var Mǫgnús í konungs garði en Hǫkon í Skúlagarði niðr frá Klémetskirkju, ok helt svá jólavist. Þá nam Hǫkon af jólagjafar ok skyldir allar ok landaura gjald við Þrœndi ok við Upplendinga alla þá er við hónum tóku, ok bœtti þar í mót mǫrgu ǫðru rétt landsmanna. En þá tók fyr þessa sǫk hugr Mǫgnúss at óróask, er hann þóttisk hafa minna af landi ok lands skǫttum en faðir hans hafði haft eða fǫðurbróðir eða forellar.[a] Þótti hónum sinn hlutr eigi síðr upp gefinn í þessi gjǫf þeim til sœmðar en Hǫkonar, þóttisk í því óvirðr ok mishaldinn af frænda sínum ok rǫ́ðum þeira Þóris beggja. Varð þeim ok á því mikill uggr, hversu Magnúsi myndi líka, fyr því at hann helt allan vetrinn .vij. langskipum í opinni vǫk í Kaupangi. En um várit náliga kyndilmessu þá lagði hann braut á náttarþeli ok tjǫlduðum skipum ok ljós undir, ok lagði til Hefringar, bjó þar of nóttina, ok gerði elda stóra á landi uppi. En þá hugði Hǫkon ok lið þat er í bœnum var at þat væri gǫrt til svika, ok lét blása liði út, ok sótti allr Kaupangrs lýðr til, ok vǫru í samnaði[b] of nóttina. En um morguninn er lýsti, er Mǫgnús sá allsherjar lið á Eyrunum, þá helt hann út ór firðinum ok svá suðr í Golaþingslǫg.

XLVII. ⟨E⟩n Hǫkon byrjaði ferð sína í Vík austr, ok helt mót í Kaupangi áðr ok sat á hesti ok hét ǫllum mǫnnum vingan ok svá bað, kvað sér vera skugga á vilja frænda síns. Ok allir menn hétu hónum vingan með góðum vilja ok fylgð ef þyrfti. Ok fylgði hónum lýðr allr undir Steinbjǫrg út, en hann fluttisk þá til fjalls upp ok fór dag einn eftir rjúpu einni er flaug undan hónum er hann reið. Þá varð

---

[a] *more normally* forellrar (*cf. p. 20 above*), *but cf.* forella(r), *pp. 66 and 74 below* (*see also Seip 1955, 279*).
[b] *written* sampnaþe.

was then in his late twenties—and both ruled one winter and spent it in Niðaróss, Magnús in the king's residence and Hákon in Skúlagarðr,[128] down from Klémetskirkja,[129] and there he celebrated the Christmas feast. Hákon abolished all Christmas dues, duties and land taxes for those Þrœndir and Upplendingar who acknowledged him as king, and in return for this he enhanced the people's rights in many other ways. Magnús became uneasy at this, because he felt the income from his lands and taxes to be less than that of his father, his uncle and his forebears. He felt that what was rightfully his, no less than Hákon's own, had been given up to the honour of the Þrœndir and Upplendingar. He felt dishonoured and wronged by his cousin and by his and Þórir's schemes.

They greatly feared Magnús's response to these measures, because the whole winter he kept seven longships at an opening in the ice at Kaupangr. But that spring, near Candlemas, he left during the night with the ships tented and with lights under the tents and made for Hefring.[130] He stayed there the night and built huge fires ashore. Hákon and the men who were in the town suspected treachery and called together an army, and all the townsmen gathered together and remained in readiness throughout the night. But in the morning when it got light and Magnús saw the public troops on Eyrar, he sailed out of the fjord and south to Gulaþingslǫg.

XLVII. Hákon held a meeting in Kaupangr before undertaking the journey eastward to Vík. He sat on horseback and promised every man friendship and asked the same in return and said he was unsure of his cousin's intentions. All willingly promised him friendship and, if necessary, support. All the people accompanied him up to Steinbjǫrg. He then went onto the mountain.[131] One day he followed a ptarmigan which flew away from him as he rode. And he

hann sjúkr ok fekk banasótt ok andaðisk þar á fjallinu, ok
kvǫmu á hálfs mánaðar fresti aftr tíðindin til Kaupangs.
Ok menn skyldu ganga í móti líki hans, ok gekk allr lýðr
á móti ok flestr allr grátandi, þvíat allir menn unnu hónum
hugǫstum, en lík hans var niðr sett í Kristskirkju.

XLVIII. ⟨E⟩n eftir fráfall Hǫkonar þá mátti Þórir eigi
víkva skapi sínu til Mǫgnúss, er þá tók við ríki, ok reisti
upp mann þann er Sveinn var kallaðr, sunr Haralds flettis,
fyr ofmetnaðar sakar, ok efldusk af Upplǫndum ok kvǫmu
niðr í Raumsdali ok á Sunnmœri, ok ǫfluðu þar skipa ok
heldu norðr í Þrǫndheim síðan. En þá er Sigurðr ullstrengr
spurði ok margir aðrir konungs vinir þessa uppreist Steigar-
Þóris ok fjándskap, þá sǫfnuðu þeir með ǫrvarskurð ǫllu
liði í móti Þóri er þeir mǫttu, ok stefndu því liði til Viggjar.
En Sveinn ok Þórir heldu þangat liði sínu, ok bǫrðusk við
þá Sigurð ok nǫðu uppgǫngu ok urðu øfri ok veittu mikit
mannspell. En Sigurðr flýði á fund konungs Mǫgnúss, er
þeir fluttusk til Kaupangs, ok hvarfuðu í firðinum þeir
Þórir eftir. En þá er þeir Þórir vǫru búnir ór firðinum ok
lagt skipum sínum í Hefring,[a] þá kom Mǫgnús konungr
útan í fjǫrðinn. En þeir Þórir lǫgðu skipum sínum yfir á
Vagnvíkastrǫnd, ok flýðu af skipum ok kvǫmu niðr í dal
þeim er heitir Þexdalr í Seljuhverfi, ok var Þórir borinn í
bǫrum yfir fjallit. Sǫfnuðu[b] skipum síðan ok fluttusk á
Hǫlogaland, en konungrinn Mǫgnús eftir þeim, ok sá hvárr
flokkrinn annan á firði þeim er Harmr heitir. Lǫgðu hinir
síðan til Hesjutúna. Þeir Þórir hugðusk hafa fengit meginland,
en þat var ey, ok urðu þar margir handteknir með Steigar-Þóri,
en hann sjálfr síðan hengðr í hólmi þeim er Vambarhólmr
heitir. Þá mælti Þórir, er hann sá gálgann: 'Ill eru ill rǫð,' ok
kvað þetta áðr hann væri hengðr ok snaran látin á hálsinn:

[a] í Hefring] *thus also* Morkinskinna *and* Fagrskinna; Heimskringla *has* við Hefring, *which seems more logical.*
[b] *after this* liþi *is written, but with points underneath to indicate deletion.*

then fell ill and this was his death-sickness and he died there on the mountain. Word reached Kaupangr a fortnight later. It was requested that the people should go to meet his body and all the townspeople went, nearly all of them crying, for all men had heartfelt love for him. His body was buried in Kristskirkja.

XLVIII. But after the death of Hákon, Þórir could not support Magnús, who then took over the kingdom, and he arrogantly put forward a man called Sveinn, the son of Haraldr flettir.[132] They gathered support in Upplǫnd and came to Raumsdalr and Sunnmœrr and there obtained ships, proceeding then north to Þrándheimr. When Sigurðr ullstrengr and many others of the king's friends received word of Steigar-Þórir's rebellion and enmity they summoned all the forces they could against him and turned their army towards Vigg. Sveinn and Þórir brought their army there and fought Sigurðr, and they succeeded in getting ashore and won the victory, killing many men. Sigurðr fled to King Magnús, and Þórir and his men sailed to Kaupangr and there sailed back and forth in the fjord, waiting. When they had positioned their ships by Hefring and were ready to sail out of the fjord King Magnús sailed into it. But Þórir and his men took their ships over to Vagnvíkastrǫnd[133] and there left them and they came down to the valley called Þexdalr in Seljuhverfi. Þórir was carried over the mountain on a litter.[134] Thereafter they gathered ships and went to Hálogaland, but King Magnús came after them and the armies sighted each other on the fjord called Harmr. Þórir and his men then went to Hesjutún. They thought they had reached the mainland, but it was an island, and there Steigar-Þórir was captured and many with him. Þórir himself was then hanged on an islet called Vambarhólmr. When he saw the gallows he said: 'Bad is a bad plan,' and before he was hanged and the noose put round his neck he spoke this verse:

6. Vǫrum félagar fjórir forðum, einn við stýri.

En Egill Áskelssunr á Forlandi, enn vaskasti maðr, var ok þar drepinn ok hengðr með Þóri, þvíat hann vildi eigi flýja frá Ingibjǫrgu konu sinni, Ǫgmundardóttur, systur Skopta. Þá mælti konungrinn Mǫgnús, er hann Egill hekk á gálganum: 'Illa koma hónum góðir frændr í hald.' En Sveinn flýði í haf út ok svá til Danmarkar, ok var þar til þess er hann kom í sætt við Eystein konung, sun Mǫgnúss, er hann tók í sætt ok gørði skutilsvein sinn ok hafði í kærleik ok í virktum. En Mǫgnús konungr hafði þá ríki einn saman ok ankannalaust, ok friðaði vel fyr landi sínu, ok eyddi ǫllum víkingum ok útilegumǫnnum, ok var maðr herskár ok rǫskr ok starfsamr, ok líkari í ǫllu Haraldi fǫðurfeðr sínum í skaplyndi heldur en fǫður sínum. Allir vǫru þeir miklir menn ok fríðir sýnum.[a]

XLIX. ⟨M⟩ǫgnús fór margar herfarar ok fekk þat fyrst til ákalls á Gautland austr, at hann kvað Dal ok Véar ok Vǫrðynjar með réttu eiga at liggja til Nóregs, kvað sína forella haft hafa forðum, ok settisk konungrinn síðan við landamæri með miklu liði ok bjó í tjǫldum, ok hugðisk til áreiðar á Gautland. En þá er Ingi konungr frá þat, þá samnaði hann brátt liði saman ok stefndi á fund hans. En þá er konunginum Mǫgnúsi kom sǫnn njósn of ferð hans, þá eggjuðu hǫfðingjar aftrhvarfs, en hann þekkðisk eigi þat, ok helt á mót konunginum Inga fyrr en hann verði ok á náttarþeli ok gerði mikinn mannskaða, en konungrinn Ingi freltisk með flótta. En síðan var máli snúit til sættar, ok tók Mǫgnús konungr Margrétu, dóttur Inga konungs, ok þessar eignir með er hann kallaði áðr til.

---

[a] Allir . . . sýnum] *written twice in the margin, the first for the most part erased.*

6. Four fellows were we once,
   one at the helm.[135]

Egill Áskelsson from Forland, a very brave man, was also killed and hanged there with Þórir because he would not leave his wife Ingibjǫrg Ǫgmundardóttir, Skopti's sister. As Egill hung from the gallows, King Magnús said: 'Good kin are of little benefit to him.'[136]

Sveinn fled out to sea and on to Denmark and remained there till he was reconciled with Magnús's son King Eysteinn, who made peace with him and made him his page[137] and held him in favour and affection.

King Magnús ruled alone and uncontested, kept his land in peace and rid the country of all vikings and outlaws. He was a warlike man, doughty and industrious, and in disposition he was in every respect more like his grandfather Haraldr than like his father. They were all tall and handsome men.

XLIX. Magnús went on many campaigns. His first claim was eastwards against Gautland, saying that Dalr, Véar and Varðynjar rightfully belonged to Norway, as his forefathers had ruled them in the past. He took up position at the border with a great army camped in tents and intended to mount an invasion of Gautland. When King Ingi[138] received word of this he soon gathered together an army and went to meet him.

But when King Magnús heard true report of his movements, the chieftains urged that they turn back, but he would not consent to this and attacked King Ingi earlier than he expected, and at night, and killed many men, but King Ingi escaped through flight. Afterwards they came to an agreement whereby Magnús took King Ingi's daughter Margrét and with her those lands to which he had earlier laid claim.[139]

L. ⟨Í⟩ þessi herfǫr vǫ́ru með Mǫgnúsi konungi Ǫgmundr Skoptasunr, Sigurðr Sigurðarsunr ok Sigurðr ullstrengr ok margir aðrir. [E]n eftir þetta leitar konungrinn Mǫgnús í Orkneyjar með liði. Vǫ́ru þá með hónum þessir hǫfðingjar: Dagr, faðir Gregóris, Víðkuðr Jóanssunr, Úlfr Ranasunr, bróðir Sigurðar, fǫður Nikulauss, ok margir aðrir stórir hǫfðingjar. Tekr hann í Orkneyjum síðan jarlinn Erlend með sér ok Mǫgnús, sun hans, áttján vetra gamlan, er nú er heilagr, lagðisk út síðan í hernað fyr Skotland ok fyr Bretland, ok drap í þeiri jarl þann er Hugi hét enn digri. Hann ⟨var⟩ skotinn í auga, ok gekk þar af til heljar. En hinn er skotit hafði kastaði boganum til konungs, at því er sumir segja, ok kvað svá at orði, at 'heill skotit herra!'— kenndi þat skot konunginum. Vendi heim ór þessi herfǫr með hlǫðnum skipum gulls ok silfrs ok gersima.

LI. ⟨E⟩n fǫ́m vetrum síðarr gørðisk hann vestr til Írlands með skipastóli ok ferr með miklu liði ok ætlar at vinna landit ok vann nekkvern lut í fyrstunni. Dirfðisk hann af því ok gerðisk síðan óvarari, með því at í fyrstu gekk hónum með vildum, sem Haraldi fǫðurfeðr hans er hann fell á Englandi. Drógu hann til lífláts ok in sǫmu svik, þvíat Írir sǫmnuðu á mót Mǫgnúsi konungi óvígjum her með leynd umb aftaninn fyr Barthólómeúsmessu, þá er þeir gengu frá skipum á land upp at hǫggva strandhǫgg. Fundu þeir eigi fyrr en liðit kom á miðal þeira ok skipanna, en þeir konungrinn lítt við búnir at herklæðum, þvíat konungrinn var upp genginn í silkihjúp ok hjálm á hǫfði, sverði gyrðr ok spjót í hendi, ⟨í⟩ stighosum—svá var hann oft vanr—ok fell í þessi Mǫgnús konungr ok mikit lið með hónum. Þar heitir á Úlaðsstíri er hann fell, ok Eyvindr Finn[s]sunr fell þar með hónum ok margir aðrir stórir hǫfðingjar. Var Víðkuðr staddr næst konunginum ok fekk

L. With King Magnús on this expedition were Ǫgmundr Skoptason, Sigurðr Sigurðarson, Sigurðr ullstrengr and many others.

Thereafter King Magnús made for Orkney with an army. These chieftains were with him: Dagr, the father of Gregóríús, Víðkunnr Jóansson, Úlfr Hranason, the brother of Sigurðr, who was Nikulaus's father, and many other important chieftains.[140] In Orkney he took with him Jarl Erlendr and his eighteen-year-old son Magnús, who is now a saint.[141] They harried the coasts of Scotland and Wales, and on that expedition killed a jarl named Hugi digri.[142] He was shot in the eye and died as a result. The one who shot the arrow threw the bow to the king and, according to some accounts, remarked: 'Well shot, Sir,' thus attributing it to the king. Magnús returned home from this expedition with his ships laden with gold, silver and costly things.

LI. A few years later he set out west to Ireland with a fleet of ships, taking a large force of men, intending to conquer that country.[143] He won a part of it straight away and as a result grew bolder and then became more unwary, because all went well for him in the beginning, just as it had for his grandfather Haraldr, when he fell in England. And the same treachery drew him to his death, for the Irish raised in secrecy an overwhelming army against King Magnús on St Bartholomew's Eve,[144] when he and his men had gone ashore from their ships to make a strand-raid. The first thing they knew was that the army had come between them and their ships. The king and his men had little armour, for the king had gone ashore wearing a silk doublet and on his head a helmet, girt with a sword and with a spear in his hand, and he wore gaiters, as was his custom. King Magnús fell on this expedition and many men with him. Where he died is called Ulster, and Eyvindr Finnsson[145] died there with him, along with many other great chieftains.

sér þrjú,[a] en þá er konungrinn Mǫgnús sá sér vísan bana, þá bað hann Víðkunn hjálpa sér með flótta, ok sótti hann þá ok þat lið annat sem undan komsk til skipa, ok svá heim í land aftr. Fekk hann síðan af því mikit metorð af sunum hans, at hann hafði svá vel þar haft sik. Þá var Mýrjartak Kondjálfasunr yfirkonungr á Írlandi. Hans dóttur átti Sigurðr Mǫgnússunr nekkvera stund. Hón hét Bjaðmunjo. Mǫgnús berleggr vas alls konungr .x. vetr.

LII. ⟨E⟩n eftir Mǫgnús þá stíga[b] til ríkis synir hans þrír, Eysteinn ok Sigurðr ok Óláfr, allir góðir menn ok listuligir, róir menn, hœgsamir ok friðsamir, ok er mart gótt ok dýrligt frá þeim at segja. Var Óláfs þó of litla ríð við freistat, þvíat hann lifði eigi lengr en tólf vetr eftir fráfall fǫður síns, andaðisk í Kaupangi seytján vetra gamall, ok var jarðaðr í Kristskirkju, ok hǫrmuðu allir menn hans fráfall. En í fyrstu, er þeir brœðr sitja í ríki þrír, Eysteinn ok Sigurðr ok Óláfr, þá fýsir Sigurð at ferðask ór landi til Jórsala með ráði brœðra sinna ok bǫztu manna í landinu. En at kaupa sér guðs miskunn ok vinsæld við alþýðu, þá tóku þeir allir brœðr af áþjánar ok ánauðir ok illar álǫgur er frekir konungar ok jarlar hǫfðu lagt á lýðinn, sem fyrr var sagt.

LIII. ⟨N⟩ú leiddu þeir brœðr svá ánauði til frelsis, en síðan ferðaðisk Sigurðr konungr ór landi til Jórsala með sex tøgu skipa fjórum vetrum eftir fráfall Mǫgnúss fǫður síns, ok hafði með sér fjǫlmennt ok góðmennt—ok þó þá eina er fara vildu—sat á Englandi enn fyrsta vetrinn, en annan út til Jórsala, ok sætti þar mikilli tígn, ok þá þar dýrligar gǫrsimar.

---

[a] *written* þrio.
[b] tiga *repeated, but with points underneath to indicate deletion.*

Víðkunnr stood nearest to the king and received three wounds, and King Magnús asked him to save himself by flight when he saw for certain that he himself would die. Víðkunnr and the others who managed to escape returned to their ships and then back home to Norway. For having behaved so well Víðkunnr later received great honour from the sons of Magnús.

At that time Mýrjartak Kondjálfason ruled as high king in Ireland. Sigurðr Magnússon was married to his daughter for a time. Her name was Bjaðmunjo.[146] Magnús berleggr was king ten years in all.

LII. After Magnús, his three sons Eysteinn, Sigurðr and Óláfr succeeded to the kingdom. They were all good men, handsome, gentle men, quiet and peace-loving, and there is much good and splendid to be said about them. Trial was made of Óláfr only a short time, however, for he lived but twelve winters after his father's death. He died in Kaupangr at the age of seventeen and was buried in Kristskirkja. His death was mourned by all.

But in the beginning, when the three brothers Eysteinn, Sigurðr and Óláfr, ruled, Sigurðr got the urge to leave Norway and travel to Jerusalem, and his brothers and the most important men in the country agreed to this.

To gain for themselves the mercy of God and the favour of the people, all the brothers abolished harsh and oppressive measures and onerous taxes which impudent kings and jarls had imposed on the people, as has been told.[147]

LIII. In this way the brothers now changed oppression to freedom. Then four years after the death of his father Magnús, King Sigurðr travelled abroad to Jerusalem with sixty ships. He had with him a large and goodly company, though only those who wanted to go. He stayed in England the first winter and spent the next on the journey to Jerusalem, where he was received with great honour and given splendid treasures.[148]

LIV. ⟨B⟩eiddisk konungrinn af krossinum helga ok ǫðlaðisk, en eigi þó fyrr en tólf menn ok sjálfr hann enn þrettándi svǫru at hann skyldi fremja kristni með ǫllum mætti sínum, ok erkibyskupsstól koma í land ef hann mætti, ok at krossinn skyldi þar vera sem inn helgi Óláfr hvíldi, ok at hann skyldi tíund fremja ok sjálfr gera. Ok helt hann þessu sumu, þvíat tíund framði hann, en hinu brá hann, er til mikils geigs myndi standa, ef eigi hefði guð þann geig með jartegnum leyst; reisti kirkju við landsenda ok setti þar krossinn náliga undir vald heiðinna manna—sem síðan gafsk—hugði þar til lands gæzlu ok varð at misræðum. Kómu þar heiðnir menn ok brenndu kirkjuna, tóku krossinn ok kennimanninn ok fluttu[a] hvártveggja braut. Kom síðan at inum heiðnum hiti svá mikill at þeir þóttusk náliga brenna, ok óttuðusk þann atburð sem skyssi, en prestrinn segir þeim at sá bruni kømr af guðs megni ok af kraft ens [he]lga[b] kross, ok þeir skutu þá báti ok settu bæði til lands, krossinn ok prestinn. Ok með því at prestinum þótti eigi heilt at setja hann annat sinni undir sama váða, þá flutti hann krossinn á launungu norðr til staðarins til ins helga Óláfs, sem hann var svarinn, ok nú er hann síðan.

LV. ⟨E⟩n mart var ok annat gótt í ferð hans. Sigr vann hann á nekkverum borgum heiðnum, ok hét til tǫku einnar þeirar at fella af kjǫtǫtu[c] á þváttdegi í Nóregi. Til Miklagarðs fór hann ok hlaut þar mikla tígn af viðrtǫku keisarans ok stórar gjafir, ok lét þar eftir til minna þarvistar sinnar skip sín, ok tók af skipi sínu einu hǫfuð mikil ok fjárverð ok setti á Pétrskirkju. En heim í Nóreg sœkir hann um Ungeraland ok Saxland, of Danmǫrk eftir þrjá vetr er hann fór ór landi,

---

[a] *MS* flvctu.
[b] *added in the margin; now scarcely legible.*
[c] *first element written* quiot, *over which a* k *has been added.*

LIV. The king asked for a fragment of the True Cross and was given one, but not until twelve men, and he himself the thirteenth, had sworn that he would advance Christianity with all his might and establish an archbishop's see in his country if he could, and furthermore that the Cross would be kept where St Óláfr lay, and that a tithe, which he himself was to pay as well, would be levied. And he kept to some of this, for he imposed a tithe, but the rest he disregarded, and this would have caused great harm had not God intervened miraculously. Sigurðr built a church on the frontier,[149] and put the Cross there, almost in the heathen's hands—as later happened[150]—thinking this would act to protect the country, but this proved ill-advised, for the heathens came, burned the church and captured the Cross and the priest and took both away. Thereafter such a great heat came upon the heathens that they thought themselves almost burning and this terrified them as a bad omen, and the priest told them that this fire came from God's might and the power of the Holy Cross, so they put out a dinghy and put both the Cross and the priest ashore. The priest thought it unwise to subject the Cross a second time to such danger and moved it in secrecy north to the place where it had been sworn on oath that it would be kept, to the shrine of St Óláfr, and there it has remained ever since.

LV. There were many other good things on Sigurðr's journey. He won victories over several heathen towns and vowed to ban the eating of meat on Saturdays in Norway if he took one of them.

He went to Mikligarðr and received much honour there from the emperor's reception and great gifts. He left his ships there as a memorial of his visit. He took off one of his ships several great and costly figure-heads and put them on the church of St Peter. He returned to Norway through Hungary, Saxony and Denmark three years after

ok fagnaði allr lýðr kvǫmu hans. Þá var hann tvítugr er hann kom aftr í land ór þessi ferð, ok var orðinn enn tíðasti. Vetri var Eysteinn ellri þeira brœðra, en Óláfr þá .xij. vetra gamall. Eru enn margir hǫstaðir skrýddir af þeim gǫrsimum er þá flutti Si . . .[a]

LVI. . . . ok lǫgðu vistagjald á Smálǫnd, .xv.c. nauta, ok tóku við krisni.[b] Ok vendi síðan Sigurðr konungr heim með mǫrgum stórum gǫrsimum[c] ok fjárhlutum er hann hafði aflat í þeiri, ok var sjá leiðangr kallaðr Kalmarna[d] leiðangr. Sjá leiðangr var sumri[e] fyrr en myrkr et mikla. Gǫrðisk þá gótt of hans daga bæði of ár ok of margfalda aðra gœzku, nema þat einu var at, at hann mátti varla skapi sínu stýra, þá er at hónum kom óhœgyndi, þá er á leið upp. En þó þótti hann allra konunga dýrligastr vera ok merkiligastr, ok allra helzt [oo][f] af ferð sinni. Hann var ok inn ríkuligsti maðr, ok manna hæstr, sem faðir hans ok forellar. Unni hann lýð sínum, en lýðrinn hónum, ok birti hann ǫst sinni með[g] þessum kviðlingi:

7. Búendr þykkja mér baztir,
byggt land ok friðr standi.

LVII. En af því trausti er[h] hann þóttisk hafa af ástsemð lýðsins, þá lét hann sér lifanda sverja Magnúsi syni sínum landit í ǫllum Nóregi. Hann var frillu[i] sunr, ok allra manna væ⟨n⟩str þeira er verit hafi.

LVIII. ⟨E⟩n eftir þetta þá sœkir sá maðr vestan af Írlandi er Haraldr hét gillikrist, ok kallaðisk sunr Mǫgnúss ok

---

[a] *there is a leaf missing in the MS here.*
[b] *i. e.* kristni.
[c] *written* geRsimum; ør *has been added over the line.*
[d] *MS* carlmarna (*perhaps a folk-etymology rather than a scribal error*).
[e] *written* sumpri, *the* p *perhaps corrected from* r.
[f] *probably the word* af.
[g] *MS adds* a/st siNi, *struck out.*
[h] *MS* en.
[i] *the first* l *has apparently been 'corrected' from* þ.

he had left, and all the people rejoiced at his return. He was twenty when he returned to Norway after this journey and he had become most famous.

Eysteinn was a year older than Sigurðr, and Óláfr was then twelve years old.

There are still many holy places adorned with the treasures King Si[gurðr] brought . . .[151]

LVI. . . . and levied a food-tax of fifteen-hundred cattle on Smálǫnd; and the people accepted Christianity.[152] King Sigurðr then returned home with much treasure and booty gathered on that expedition. It was called the Kalmarnar expedition and took place the summer before the great darkness.[153]

Sigurðr's time was a good one, both in terms of harvests and many other beneficial things, with the one exception that he could hardly control his temper when he suffered attacks[154] as he grew older. But he was nevertheless regarded as the most splendid and remarkable of all kings, and in particular because of his journey. He was also a very fine-looking man and very tall, as his father and forefathers had been. He loved his people, and they him, and he expressed his affection in this verse:

> 7. Farmers I find best;
> may farmed land and peace endure.

LVII. Because of the support he felt he had through the people's love, Sigurðr had the whole of Norway swear allegiance to his son Magnús while he still lived. Magnús was the son of a mistress and was the finest man there has ever been.[155]

LVIII. But after this there came a man from the west from Ireland named Haraldr gillikrist,[156] and he claimed to be

bróðir Sigurðar, bauð til þess sǫnnur, ok konungrinn þekkðisk, meir með einvilja sínum en með vitra manna ráði, ok trað Haraldr .ix. plógjǫrn sindrandi, ok varð skírr, var síðan í góðu yfirlæti með brœðr sínum, þvíat maðrinn var vaskr[a] [oooo] ok liðmannligr [oooo], hǫr vǫxtum ok inn vakrligsti sýnum. ⟨E⟩n eiðar stóðu sem unnir vǫru um Mǫgnús. Haraldr vann ok eið áðr hann næði skírslum at hann skyldi ekki til ríkis kalla meðan Mǫgnús lifði, ok vildi konungrinn með þeim eiðstaf staðfesta eið lýðsins ok ríki sunar síns ok váða úti byrgja ok stefja manntjón. En þessar skírslir vǫru gervar á Sæheimi, ok sýndisk mǫnnum skírslirnar[b] frekeflt,[c] af því at hann bar til faðernis en eigi til ríkis, er hann hafði fyrir svarit. En brátt eftir þetta andaðisk konungrinn austr í Ǫsló, en Haraldr ok Mǫgnús vǫru í Túnsbergi, ok vǫru þegar orð gǫr út til Mǫgnúss, ok hann hvataði ferð sinni inn til Ǫslóar ok komsk hann svá at gørsimum. En líkamr Sigurðar konungs var jarðaðr í Hallvarðskirkju, þá er hann hafði alls ráðit Nóregi .vij. vetr ok .xx.

LIX. ⟨N⟩ú vill Mǫgnús einn í ríki setjask, sem hónum vísar með réttu tilskipan fǫður hans ok eiðr alþýðu, en Haraldi gezk eigi at því ok kallar til hálfs ríkis, ok vill hvárki muna eiða sína né skipan bróður síns. Ok gerisk nú á fyrstu .vij. nóttum með þeim ósamþykki, ok dregsk nú í tvá staði hirðin ok hǫfðingjar ok alþýða, ok fekksk Haraldi af því œrit lið ok . . .[d]

LX. . . . fóstrar þeira, ok hǫfðu þeir eina hirð báðir, Ingi konungr ok Sigurðr konungr, en Eysteinn konungr einn sér. Ok er þessir hǫfðingjar ǫnduðusk allir, [ooooooo] er

[a] *written over an erasure in different ink.*
[b] *MS* scirslirner.
[c] *written* frechelft; *this is a nonce-word; one might have expected the form* frekefldar, *though maybe a word like* gǫrvar *or* framðar *should be understood or supplied.*
[d] *here there are probably four leaves missing, after which a new hand begins.*

the son of Magnús and Sigurðr's brother, and offered to give evidence of this.[157] The king gave him leave to do so, more because it was his will than by the advice of his counsellors. Haraldr walked over nine glowing hot ploughshares and was clean, and was afterwards made much of by his brother, for he was valiant and doughty, tall and very lively in appearance. But the oaths regarding Magnús still stood.

Before he was allowed to submit to ordeal, Haraldr had also sworn an oath that he would make no claim to the throne while Magnús lived. With this oath the king wished to confirm the oath of the people and thus secure his son's rule and so keep trouble at bay and prevent loss of life.

These ordeals were carried out at Sæheimr,[158] and people thought them excessive, for Haraldr had submitted to ordeal in order to prove his paternity and not his right to the throne, which he had already forsworn.

Soon after this the king died east in Oslo, while Haraldr and Magnús were in Túnsberg, and word was immediately sent to Magnús and he hurried to Oslo and in this way gained the treasure. The body of King Sigurðr was buried in Hallvarðskirkja, when he had ruled Norway twenty-seven winters in all.

LIX. It was then Magnús's intention to rule alone, as his father's arrangement and the oath of the people entitled him to, but Haraldr was not pleased with this and laid claim to half the kingdom, choosing to remember neither his oaths nor his brother's arrangement. During the first week there arose disagreement between them, and the court, the chieftains and the people split into two groups. Haraldr gained plenty of support as a result and . . .[159]

LX. . . . their fosterfathers. King Ingi and King Sigurðr shared one following together and King Eysteinn[160] had one of his own, but soon after, with the deaths of all the

með sínum ráðum hǫfðu [ooooooooo] drengiliga stýrt ríkinu með þeim eptir landslǫgum þeira—[Sáða-Gyrðr][a] ok Ǫmundi, Þjóstólfr Ǫlasunr ok Óttarr birtingr, er átti Ingiríði, móður Inga konungs, ok Ǫgmundr sviptir ok Ǫgmundr dengir, bróðir Erlings skakka, sunr Kyrpinga-Orms, er bæði var miklu tígnari at metorðum Erlingi meðan þeir lifðu báðir ok ellri at vetratali—þá skilðu þeir brœðr, Sigurðr ok Ingi, bráðliga eptir þat hirð sína. Sigurðr konungr var mikill maðr vexti ok liðmannligr, ramr at afli, marglyndr ok málsnjallr, vandlyndr ok vanstilltr, hraustr ok glaðr. Eysteinn konungr var hár maðr ok styrkr [oooo] ok bermǫlugr, slœgvitr, undirhyggjumaðr, fastr ok fégjarn, svartr ok skrúfhárr. Ingi konungr var hvítr maðr ok vænn í andliti, vanheill, ryggbrotinn ok visnaði fótr annarr, svá at hann fór mjǫk haltr, þýðr ok þekkr við sína menn. Sigurðr konungr var ofstopamaðr mikill of alla hluti ok óeiramaðr þegars hann óx upp, ok svá þeir Eysteinn báðir brœðr, ok var þat nær sanni nøkkvi er Eysteinn var, en hann þótti þó allra fégjarnastr þeira. Ingi konungr var vinsæll við alþýðu. Ok nǫkkuru eptir andlát rǫ́ðuneytis konunganna gerðisk sá atburðr at maðr hét Geirsteinn ok átti .ij. sonu, Hjarranda ok Hísing, ok hans dóttir var frilla Sigurðar konungs ok þeir í kærleikum við hann. Geirsteinn var óeirðarmaðr mikill ok ranglátr, sat í trausti konungsins. Skammt[b] í frá hónum bjó gǫfug ekkja er Gyða hét, systir Ragnhild⟨a⟩r, er átti Dagr Eilífssunr austan ór Vík. Hón var skǫrungr mikill. Geirsteinn ferr opt á hennar fund ok vill gjarna fá hennar ǫst, en þat var ǫn hennar vilja, ok þá ylmðisk[c] hann í móti ok segr því munu

---

[a] *there is an erasure here of about nine letters*; this is Storm's reading (Ágrip *1880, 124*).

[b] *written* scampt.

[c] *MS* vlinþsc, *suggesting that the scribe did not understand his exemplar.*

following chieftains, who had, through their counsel, governed the kingdom with them bravely and in accordance with the law of the land: [Sáða-Gyrðr], Ámundi, Þjóstólfr Álason, Óttarr birtingr—who was married to Ingiríðr, King Ingi's mother—Ǫgmundr sviptir and Ǫgmundr dengir—who was the brother of Erlingr skakki Kyrpinga-Ormsson and both older than Erlingr in years and the one who achieved by far the greater honour while they both lived—the brothers Sigurðr and Ingi divided their court.[161]

King Sigurðr was a tall man and doughty, strong, temperamental and eloquent, irascible and intemperate, valiant and merry. King Eysteinn was tall, strong and outspoken, a crafty, guileful man, mean and miserly, dark and curly-haired. King Ingi was fair and had a handsome face, poor in health, with a broken back and one withered leg, so that he walked with a great limp.[162] He was kindly and amiable towards his men.

King Sigurðr was an overbearing man in every way and an unruly man when he grew up. And so was his brother Eysteinn, though it was rather more true in his case for he was considered the most avaricious of them all. King Ingi was popular with the people.

A little after the deaths of the kings' counsellors, this came to pass:[163] there was a man named Geirsteinn who had two sons, Hjarrandi and Hísingr, and a daughter who was the mistress of King Sigurðr, and they were on intimate terms with him. Geirsteinn was an unruly man and unjust. He was in the king's favour.

A short way away from him lived a noble widow named Gyða. Her sister was Ragnhildr, who was married to Dagr Eilífsson from Vík in the east. She was a woman of outstanding character and Geirsteinn often went to see her and was eager to gain her love, but she was unwilling. As a result he went into a rage and said that refusing him

vera misráðit. Er þat et fyrsta ráð hans ok bragð at hann lætr reka fé hennar í akra sína ok gaf þar fyrir sakar henni, ok þar með lætr hann með kappi fylgja sínu fé í hennar akra, ok gera henni miklar meizlur á marga vega. Ok er hón sér hans óþokka svá mikinn ok sér skaða gǫrvan, þá mælir hón við sína vini at hón missir mjǫk gǫfgra sinna vina ok forsjámanna, er hón skal svá marga vega óvirð vera. Þá sagði sá maðr henni er Gyrðr hét—hann var þar upp fœddr við henni ok góðrar ættar ok vaskligr maðr—'Fróva,' segr hann, 'þat er satt er þú mælir. Mikit vanhald hefir þú af þessum manni beðit, en sjǫ́m vér at hér til víkr þú máli er vérrum at hafa atgerðir.' Ok þat bar at einn dag er hón gekk of bœ sinn at hón sá mart fé í sínum ǫkrum ok mart gera mikinn skaða. Þá verðr hón reið, tekr eitt spjót ok hleypr út ok vendir þangat til sem féit var. Nú kømr í móti henni Gyrðr ok tekr af henni spjótit ok gengr í mót fénu ok rekr á braut ok yfir brú er á var ánni milli bœjanna, ok nú kømr í móti hónum Geirsteinn, ok hleypr þegar at hónum ok segir, at þeir hafa of dregit fram þræla, er slíkir skulu hónum jafnask, ok leggr til hans. Gyrðr berr af sér lagit ok hǫggr til hans í mót á vinstri síðu, ok veitir hónum banasár, ferr síðan á fund Gyðu ok segr svá búit. Hón hefir ok þá búit hesta .ij., annan við fé, en hónum annan til reiðar . . .[a]

---

[a] *the manuscript breaks off here.*

would prove to be a mistake. His first plan and scheme was to have all her cattle driven onto his corn-fields and lay the blame for this on her; then in retaliation he had his cattle led onto her corn-fields and in many ways caused her great injury.

When she saw how great was his malevolence, and the damage he had done her, she said to her friends how greatly she felt let down by her noble friends and guardians, that she should now be slighted in so many ways. A man named Gyrðr who had been brought up in her neighbourhood and was of good family and a brave man, then said to her: 'Lady,' he said, 'what you say is true: you have suffered very bad treatment at the hands of this man. But I see that you direct your speech to me, expecting me to act upon it.' And it happened one day as she walked round her farm, that she saw many cattle in her corn-fields and many causing great damage. She became angry and took a spear and ran out and made for where the cattle were. Gyrðr came out to meet her, took the spear from her and walked over toward the cattle, driving them away and over the bridge spanning the river that divided the farms. Geirsteinn came to meet him and ran toward him immediately, saying that they had promoted slaves too highly if people like him were to be measured against him, and he thrust at Gyrðr. Gyrðr parried the blow and struck in return on the left hand side, dealing him a death wound. He then went to see Gyða and told her what had happened. She had already prepared two horses, one with money and the other for him to ride . . .

NOTES TO THE TRANSLATION

1. According to Snorri (*Heimskringla* I 97, 122) and most of the other sources, Haraldr vows neither to cut nor comb his hair till he is king of all Norway. This vow is absent from the story as preserved here, but may have appeared in that part of the manuscript now wanting at the beginning. It is said that when Haraldr's hair finally was cut, ten years later, he was redubbed *hárfagri*, 'fine-hair'.

2. The Scandinavians retained *jól*, the name of their pre-Christian mid-winter feast, or forms of it, as the name of the Christian celebration which gradually replaced it. The Old Icelandic *jólmánuðr*, 'yule-month', was the third month of winter, lasting from mid-December to mid-January. Thus it corresponds to the OE *gēol*, the twin months around the winter solstice, a sense preserved in the modern English Yule and Yule-tide. On Old Norse–Icelandic time-reckoning generally see Þorsteinn Vilhjálmsson 1990, especially 16–24, and Árni Björnsson 1990; or, in English, Hastrup 1985, 17–49 and references there.

Jólnir as a name for Óðinn appears elsewhere, but is not common. Snorri, quoting Eyvindr skáldaspillir, gives the plural form *jólnar* as a name for the gods in general (*Edda Snorra Sturlusonar* 1931, 166). In *Flateyjarbók* (I 564), Óðinn's name is (correctly) derived from that of the feast, and not, as here, the other way round.

Viðrir, *Hár* and *Þriði* are probably the best attested of Óðinn's two hundred-odd names. *Viðrir* is related to *veðr*, 'weather', meaning 'he who rules the weather' (cf. *Flateyjarbók* I 564). *Hár(r)* and *Þriði*, 'High' (or 'Hoary', or 'One-eyed') and 'Third', appear frequently, for example in Snorri's *Gylfaginning* (*Edda Snorra Sturlusonar* 1931, 10–16 *et passim*) as two members of a much-debated pagan trinity (see Lorenz 1984, 81–83). The third member, *Jafnhár*, 'Equally High', is here omitted. On Óðinn's various names see Turville-Petre 1964, 61–63.

3. Hálfdan svarti was the son of Guðrøðr, king in Vestfold. Haraldr hárfagri was Hálfdan's son by his second wife Ragnhildr, daughter of Sigurðr hjǫrtr, king in Hringaríki (now Ringerike). According to tradition, Hálfdan was forty at the time of his death and Haraldr ten at the time of his accession (cf. *Ágrip*'s own 'by the age of twenty he was the first king to gain all Norway' and 'ten winters he fought'). Beginning with Ari fróði, the Icelandic sources—and *Ágrip*, though whether on the basis of Ari's chronology remains a point of contention—seem to reckon Haraldr's birth to have been not later than 851 or 852 (see

Íslendingabók xxxv), a date historians agree must be too early. The problems surrounding dates for the earliest kings of Norway are complex; discussion can be found in *Heimskringla* I lxxi–lxxxi; Jón Jóhannesson 1956, 26–27 (1974, 13–15); Ólafía Einarsdóttir 1964, 59–61; *Íslendingabók* xxxv–xxxviii; and Andersen 1977, 79–84.

4. In other sources (e. g. *Heimskringla* I 91–92) a Yule-feast is specified; presumably the reason for the digression on the origin of the word *jól* in the preceding paragraph.

5. There is a large mound in Ringerike called Halvdanshaugen. *Fagrskinna* (58) and *Ágrip* agree that Hálfdan was buried there, but in *Heimskringla* (I 93) and other sources his body is said to have been divided into three (or four) parts, so that one part of him could be buried in each part of his kingdom. This is not known to have been a practice in Norway in heathen times, and the story is not generally credited.

6. The place here called *Hafrsvágr* is known in other sources as *Hafrsfjǫrðr* (i. e. 'Goat's fjord' as opposed to 'bay'). Finnur Jónsson (1928, 281) suggested that the author could here have been working from a Latin source in which the name appeared as *Capri sinus*, which, being unfamiliar with the original name, he rendered back into Norse as *Hafrsvágr*.

7. *Oddmjór*, 'thin (i. e. narrow) at the point'. This poem is otherwise unknown, nor does the half-verse cited here appear elsewhere. Bjarni Einarsson (*Ágrip* 1984, xlvii; 4) suggests the name might have been applied to the poem because it was thought to end abruptly.

8. ON *Skjǫldungr*, a descendant of the legendary Skjǫldr, *Beowulf*'s Scyld Scefing, founder of the Scylding dynasty of Denmark; here used as a *heiti* (poetic synonym) for king (*Lexicon Poeticum* 510); hence my translation 'Scylding-king'.

9. *Skeiðarbrandr* was the word for the decorated piece of wood on the side of a warship's prow. It is used here to mean simply ship, and is therefore not, strictly speaking, a kenning, but rather an example of synecdoche. The author of *Ágrip* misinterprets the term, however, taking the second element as the personal name Brandr. This has been cited as evidence for Norwegian authorship, the *locus classicus* being Turville-Petre's observation that 'an educated Icelander of that day would be sufficiently well trained in scaldic diction to avoid such obvious pitfalls' (1953, 173). But even if one accepts Turville-Petre's

view of medieval Icelanders, it must be said in defence of our author—and medieval Norwegians in general—that names of this sort (genitive plus proper name) were in no way uncommon (e. g. Skalla-Grímr), whereas the term *skeiðarbrandr* appears only twice in the whole of skaldic literature, here, and in str. 7/3–4 of the poem *Hrynhenda* by Arnórr Þórðarson jarlaskáld (*Skjd.* A I 334; B I 307), as the determinant in the kenning *skyldir skeiðarbrands*, 'a sailor' (*Lexicon Poeticum* 504). There is, moreover, a general resemblance, first pointed out by Munch (*Ágrip* 1834, 274–75), between the first two lines of *Oddmjór* and the two lines in *Hrynhenda* that contain the kenning: 'skyldir [or in some manuscripts 'skjǫldungr'] stǫkk með skœðan þokka / skeiðarbrands fyr þér ór landi'. Sveinbjörn Egilsson (*Ágrip* 1841, 351) noted in addition a resemblance between the second couplet of *Oddmjór* and two lines from Arnórr's *Magnúsdrápa*, str. 7: 'Náði siklingr síðan / snjallr ok Danmǫrk allri' (*Skjd.* A I 340; B I 312), suggesting that the whole verse cited here is simply a conflation of the two.

It is also interesting, however, that the author of *Ágrip* seems to have more information on 'Brandr' than can be gleaned from the half-verse he cites, suggesting that the other half-verse—assuming there to have been one—may have contained references to Denmark and Wendland. On the other hand the author may merely have felt obliged to say more about this king Brandr and simply invented for him what seemed a probable fate for Haraldr's final enemy.

10. Haraldr's sons are also said to be twenty in *Heimskringla*, but a few of the names, and many of the nicknames, differ. *Historia Norvegiæ* names sixteen sons, thirteen of whom also appear in *Ágrip*. *Ágrip* also includes one, Eysteinn, presumably Haraldr's son by Svanhildr (see below), not mentioned by Snorri. Haraldr's various sons are listed here in roughly chronological order. Forms in *Heimskringla*, where different, are given in brackets.

By Ása Hákonardóttir: Goðormr (Guthormr), Hálfdan svarti ('the black'); *Heimskringla* also lists Hálfdan hvíti ('the white') and Sig(f)røðr, neither of whom is mentioned in *Ágrip*.

By Gyða Eiríksdóttir: Hrœrekr, Tryggvi (Sigtryggr in *Heimskringla*, both named in *Ágrip*), Fróði; *Heimskringla* also lists Þorgils (sometimes written Þorgísl), and in Snorri's Separate *Óláfs saga helga* (6) Gunnrøðr, 'whom some call Guðrøðr' (actually the same name) is said to be Haraldr's son by Gyða, together with Guthormr and

Hrœrekr. A daughter Álof (Ólof) is also mentioned in both *Heimskringla* and *Ágrip*.

By Ragnhildr Eiríksdóttir: Eiríkr blóðøx, 'blood-axe'; the cognomen is thought generally to refer to his murdering so many of his brothers—he is called *fratrum interfector* by Theodoricus (7)—but in *Fagrskinna* (79) his nickname is explained as referring to his Viking days.

By Svanhildr Eysteinsdóttir: Óláfr digrbeinn, 'stout-leg' (called *Geirstaðaálfr*, 'the elf of Geirstaðir', in *Heimskringla* (I 119); the Óláfr Geirstaðaálfr after whom this one was named also had the nickname *digrbeinn*, according to the 'Legendary Saga' (1982, 30)); Bjǫrn kaupmaðr, 'merchant', whom some call *buna*, the meaning of which is not entirely clear (Finnur Jónsson, *Ágrip* 1929, 3, note 2, gives it as 'entw. "knochenröhre" oder "klumpfuß"' (cf. Lind 1920–21, 49; Ásgeir Blöndal Magnússon 1989, 92), and Cleasby–Vigfússon 1957, 86, as 'one with the stocking hanging down his leg, ungartered'; Snorri (*Heimskringla* I 140) says that Bjǫrn's brothers called him *farmaðr* or *kaupmaðr*, 'sailor' or 'merchant'); Rǫgnvaldr, or Ragnarr, called *reykill* (*rykkill* in *Heimskringla* I 119), possibly related to *rykkja*, 'to pull' (Lind 1920–21, 299).

By Áshildr Hringsdóttir: Dagr, Hringr, Guðrøðr, called *skirja*, probably 'cow' (see Ásgeir Blöndal Magnússon 1989, 846), but tentatively related by Lind (1920–21, 327) to Norwegian (*nynorsk*) *skjerja*, 'to screech with laughter'. *Heimskringla* also mentions a daughter, Ingigerðr.

By Snjófríðr (Snæfríðr) Svásadóttir: Sigurðr hrísi, probably related to *hrísungr*, 'an illegitimate son', or, more properly, 'a son begotten in the woods' (Fritzner 1886–96, II 61; Lind 1920–21, 157–58), Hálfdan hvítbeinn, 'white-leg' (called *háleggr* or (in a verse) *Háfœta*, 'high-leg', in *Heimskringla*), Guðrøðr ljómi, 'lustre', Rǫgnvaldr (réttilbeini, 'straight-leg', in *Heimskringla*, confused with Ragnarr rykkill in *Ágrip*; see note 12 below), Hákon góði, 'the good', so called only in *Ágrip* and *Fagrskinna* (and once in *Heimskringla*), but otherwise known as Aðalsteinsfóstri, as he was brought up by King Æthelstan of England. He was not Haraldr's son by Snjófríðr according to Snorri, but by Þóra Mo(r)strstǫng.

11. Snjófríðr: Snorri (*Heimskringla* I 126) uses the variant form Snæfríðr, and calls her father Svási merely 'the Lapp', rather than 'king of the Lapps'. In *Flateyjarbók* (I 582), where there is no indication that he is Snjófríðr's father, he is said to be a dwarf.

12. The awkwardness of this passage has led some scholars to postulate the existence of a Latin source for it, in which the Norse term *seiðmaðr* was included and then glossed, presumably with something like *vocatus est seidmadr, id est propheta*. Finnur Jónsson (*Ágrip* 1929, 3) went as far as to suggest that this source might even have been the lost book of Sæmundr fróði (see Introduction, p. xv). Ulset (1983, 116–18) points out, however, that in *Ágrip* chapter XIX, where the text closely parallels that of *Historia Norvegiæ*, the author uses the loan-word *própheti*, whereas, having once translated it as *spámaðr*, he might reasonably be expected to do so again. Ulset is of the opinion that the author has confounded two persons, Rǫgnvaldr and Ragnarr, one of whom was called *skratti* (normally *seiðskratti*), the other *seiðmaðr*, from the word *seiðr*, 'charm' or 'spell'. Both words signified 'wizard' or 'warlock' in medieval usage. Loath to omit one of the terms, our author decided to define one of them more closely, although in fact they are more or less synonymous. Bjarni Einarsson (*Ágrip* 1984, xxii) has suggested instead that the author may have preferred to use the loan word *própheti* in chapter XIX in describing a man of God, having used the more normal *spámaðr* here for a pagan wizard.

13. Snorri uses the story of Snjófríðr in *Heimskringla* (I 125–27), beginning here and following *Ágrip* down to 'and the kingdom by them both' (ch. IV). Stylistically the episode differs markedly from the material surrounding it in *Heimskringla*, and it is tempting to think that Snorri recognised a good story when he heard one and felt no need to alter it. He does, however, include one piece of information not found in the story as preserved here. After the death of Snæfríðr, he says: *en litr hennar skipaðisk á engan veg, var hon jafnrjóð sem þá, er hon var kvik. Konungr sat æ yfir henni ok hugði, at hon myndi lifna*, 'but her colour changed in no way; she was as rosy-cheeked as she had been in life. The king sat always by her, and believed that she would revive.' As was mentioned above, a version of the story also appears in *Flateyjarbók* (I 582–83), one differing so significantly from that preserved in *Ágrip* that it cannot derive from it. There too we find the explanation for Haraldr's behaviour: spread over Snjófríðr after her death is the cloth *Svásanautr*—presumably the *guðvefr* and *fatnaðr* mentioned in *Ágrip* and *Heimskringla*—which is so charged with magical properties that *Haralldi konungi læitzst hennar likame suo biartr ok inniligr at hann uillde æigi iarda lata*, 'her body appeared to King Haraldr so bright and lovely that he would not have her buried'.

This must therefore have been part of the original story, and Snorri must therefore have used a version of *Ágrip* different from—and closer to the original than—the one now extant. Ólafur Halldórsson (1969) has argued that the *Flateyjarbók* version of the story derives from the poem *Snjófríðardrápa*, only the first strophe of which is cited in *Flateyjarbók* (I 582; *Skjd*. A I 5; B I 5), where it is attributed to Haraldr himself. A further five half-strophes attributed to Ormr Steinþórsson and preserved in *Edda Snorra Sturlusonar* (1931, 92, 94, 146, 147, 176; *Skjd*. A I, 415–16; B I 385) are, Ólafur maintains, also part of this same *drápa*. *Snjófríðardrápa* and the story as preserved in *Ágrip* derive from a common source. A sixth half-strophe from the same poem is found in Magnús Ólafsson's Edda; see Ólafur Halldórsson (1990).

The story's ultimate origins in folklore have been investigated by Moe (1925–27, II 168–97), who points out the relationship between the first part of the story and, for example, the tale of King Vortigern and Rowena in Geoffrey of Monmouth's *Historia Regum Britanniae* (1985–88, I 67; II 91–92), and, somewhat more distant, between the second part and the story of Snow White—called Snofrí in Norwegian versions of the tale.

14. The name Hasleyjarsund is not attested elsewhere, the strait in question being otherwise referred to as Haugasund (modern Haugesund), but Jan Ragnar Hagland (1989) has argued that Haugasund was originally not the name of the strait, but rather of a place on the coast, which was later applied to the strait itself, while Hasleyjarsund is the original name, deriving from the name of the island (Hasley, modern Hasselø, but in earlier dialect forms Hatløy).

15. Gunnhildr was probably the daughter of Gormr gamli, king of Denmark, and the sister of Haraldr blátǫnn. It was the common Icelandic view, however, that Gunnhildr was the daughter of Ǫzurr (cf. e. g. *Heimskringla* I 135, *Fagrskinna* 74, *Egils saga* 94, *Njáls saga* 11). His nickname *lafskegg*, 'dangling beard', appears also in *Fagrskinna*, but Snorri calls him *toti*, 'protuberance' (cf. English *teat* etc.), possibly with the same meaning, or in the sense of 'nose' or 'snout' (cf. Lind 1920–21, 385). In *Historia Norvegiæ* (105) Gunnhildr is identified as the daughter of Gormr. The origin of this confusion is not clear, but it may be due, at least in part, to Icelandic hostility toward Gunnhildr, whom they may have wanted to have had more humble origins. An interesting, if now somewhat dated, examination of

Gunnhildr and the legends surrounding her is offered by Sigurður Nordal (1941).

Snorri lists the sons of Eiríkr and Gunnhildr as Gamli, Guthormr, Haraldr gráfeldr ('grey-cloak'), Ragnfrøðr, Erlingr, Guðrøðr, Sigurðr slefa ('drool' or, conceivably, 'snake', see Lind 1920–21, 339; Ásgeir Blöndal Magnússon 1989, 890), all of whom are mentioned in *Ágrip*, where we also find Hálfdan, Eyvindr, and Gormr. Snorri's Guthormr is called in *Ágrip* Goðormr, an alternative form of that name; Gormr, a contracted form of Goðormr, is what one would expect Eiríkr and Gunnhildr's first-born son to have been named (i. e. after his maternal grandfather). According to Lind (1905–15, 297–98) Gamli Eiríksson is the earliest and only certain example of the name Gamli found in Norway, although there are instances of the strong form, Gamall. Nicknames could, of course, also be passed on—we have already seen an example of this in Haraldr's son Hálfdan svarti—and there are examples of nicknames becoming proper names in their own right (e. g. Magnús, from Karlamagnús = Charlemagne), so that Gamli and Gormr could have been the same person (Storm 1893, 216–17).

16. Snorri (*Heimskringla* I 147) divides the five years of Eiríkr's reign the other way, three while Haraldr lived and two thereafter, and this is the generally accepted view.

17. As was noted above, Gunnhildr's reputation is thought to have suffered at the hands of Icelandic historians. But even here, in a work apparently composed entirely in a Norwegian milieu and most probably by a Norwegian, the portrait is one of a beautiful, wicked, ambitious, treacherous and cruel woman, who practised sorcery on more than a few occasions. It may be that the author, like Theodoricus, got much of his material from Icelanders, and was prepared to accept their view of the story, but it may also be that Gunnhildr's reputation in Norway was equally notorious. Both Theodoricus (7) and *Historia Norvegiæ* (105–06), for example, blame her for Eiríkr's unpopularity.

18. According to *Heimskringla* (I 152 and II 159) and *Egils saga* (176), Eiríkr went to England by way of Orkney; Theodoricus (7) and *Historia Norvegiæ* (105), and *Ágrip* itself (chapter VII), say he went directly to England.

19. This heathen wife of Hákon's is otherwise unknown, but his daughter Þóra is mentioned in *Heimskringla* (I 192).

20. Þrœndir: men from the area of Þrándheimr, the modern Trøndelag.

21. Hákon would have been brought up a Christian at the court of his foster-father, and although he did proclaim his intention to convert the people of Norway, and may even have brought English missionaries with him to Norway, his political good sense seems to have tempered his religious fervour and there are several stories like these of his attempting to have his cake and eat it. He would drink toasts to the gods only after making the sign of the cross over the cup (*Heimskringla* I 171), or, as here, would wrap the sacrificial horse-liver in cloth so as to bite but not taste it. The chieftains would not accept these compromises and in the end Hákon worshipped as his ancestors had done. Eyvindr skáldaspillir's *Hákonarmál* (*Skjd.* A I 64–68; B I 57–60), composed in his memory, depicts his entry into Valhǫll where he is welcomed as one who has *vel um þyrmt véom* ('respected holy places').

22. The original reads: *hann setti Golaþingslǫg eftir ráðagǫrð Þorleifs spaka, er verit hafði forðum*. Here *setti* cannot mean established, as the *Gulaþingslǫg* predated Hákon's time; nor is it clear what *er verit hafði forðum* refers to (*er* could be either 'which' or 'who'). Although syntactically it could refer to Þorleifr, *er* would seem more logically to refer to *lǫg*, in which case however one would expect a plural verb, i. e. *hǫfðu*. Bjarni Einarsson (*Ágrip* 1984, li) suggests that something like *ok hagaði í flestu eptir því* could be missing between *spaka* and *er* (but cf. *Heimskringla* I 163).

23. A child would take a metronymic rather than the more common patronymic when the father was unknown, deceased or less prominent than the mother (see Hødnebø 1974, 319).

24. The Battle of Fræði (modern Frei) is generally reckoned to have been fought five years after the battle at Kǫrmt (modern Karmøy).

25. Gamli too fell at Fræði (cf. *Heimskringla* I 180–81), and the story related here may well derive from an incorrect interpretation of the name Gamlaleir, which probably means 'old clay'. Although *leir(r)* is not common as a second place-name element (see Rygh 1897–1936, Forord og indledning 65), specific incidents such as this very rarely give rise to place names (see Dalberg and Sørensen 1972–79, I 196).

26. According to Snorri (*Heimskringla* I 182), the Battle of Fitjar was fought when Hákon had been king twenty-six years, and therefore only six years after Fræði, not nine as here. The *.ix.* of the MS could be a mistake for *.vi.*, or the author could be reckoning from the Battle

of Kǫrmt, or it could simply reflect the apparent confusion among medieval historians as to the number and dates of battles between Hákon and the sons of Eiríkr. Theodoricus (10) mentions only one battle, *Historia Norvegiæ* (107) and *Fagrskinna* (81–82, 88–93) two. Snorri and *Ágrip* agree at least as to number, if not as to date.

27. The name appears in the manuscript as *scraygia* (which would be normalised 'skreygja'), but in *Heimskringla* (I 185, 189–90) and *Egils saga* (123), where he is said to be the brother of Queen Gunnhildr, he is called *skreyja*, the meaning of which may be 'a sickly-looking man' or 'a coward' (Lind 1920–21, 333). Neither seems appropriate to the character described here. Guðbrandur Vigfússon (Cleasby–Vigfússon 1957, 557) suggested 'a brayer, bragger', which Ásgeir Blöndal Magnússon (1989, 861–62) is prepared to accept. In *Historia Norvegiæ* (111) he is called simply 'Screyia'.

28. Þórálfr Skólmsson inn sterki is mentioned in a number of sources, and is everywhere said to be a man of great strength. Cf. e. g. *Heimskringla* (I 187), *Fagrskinna* (74), *Grettis saga* (187) and *Landnámabók* (257). Þórðr Sjáreksson composed a *drápa* on him, of which there are preserved three and a half verses (*Skjd*. A I 328–29; B I 302–03).

29. Eyvindr Finnsson, known as *skáldaspillir* (thought to mean 'plagiarist') was a Norwegian court poet whose *Hákonarmál*, mentioned above, through its resemblance to *Eiríksmál* (composed in honour of Eiríkr blóðøx), may have earned him his nickname.

30. Also called *Kvernbítr*, 'mill-stone biter'. Cf. *Heimskringla* I 146:

> Aðalsteinn konungr gaf Hákoni sverð þat, er hjǫltin váru ór gulli ok meðalkaflinn, en brandrinn var þó betri, þar hjó Hákon með kvernstein til augans. Þat var síðan kallat Kvernbítr. Þat sverð hefir bezt komit til Nóregs. Þat átti Hákon til dauðadags. ('King Æthelstan gave Hákon a sword with a golden hilt and haft, but the blade was even better. With it Hákon split a millstone to the eye. It was thereafter called Kvernbítr. It was the best sword ever to have come to Norway. Hákon had it until the day he died.')

31. This information is not to be found in either *Historia Norvegiæ* or Theodoricus, but Snorri (*Heimskringla* I 152–53) says that King Æthelstan sent word to Eiríkr offering him a kingdom in England. The *Anglo-Saxon Chronicle* (D) for 948 records that the Northumbrians had received Eiríkr as king in York. It is unlikely that he would have been in England much before 947, and Æthelstan died in the autumn of 939.

32. Only *Ágrip* and *Historia Norvegiæ* (106) place Eiríkr's death in Spain. Snorri (*Heimskringla* I 154) and the other Scandinavian historians, undoubtedly on the authority of *Eiríksmál* (*Fagrskinna* 79), say he died along with five other Norse kings on Stainmoor in Westmoreland (see Seeberg 1978–79). Finnur Jónsson (1920–24, II 614, n. 2) suggests *Span-* may be a corruption of *Stan-* .

33. This number is now virtually unreadable in the manuscript and could be either *.xv.* or *.xii.* A comparison with the other sources is of no help, as Snorri (*Heimskringla* I 239) gives the first and Theodoricus (10) the second as the number of years in Haraldr's reign. There is little external evidence to support either number. *Noregskonungatal* (*Flateyjarbók* II 522), which is thought, as was said, to be based on Sæmundr fróði's lost book (see Introduction, p. xvi), says that Haraldr ruled for nine years. According to *Historia Norvegiæ* (107) he ruled for fourteen years.

34. *kleypr*, written *clœpr* in the manuscript, may be another form of—or error for—*klyppr*, 'squarely-built', the form found in other sources (Lind 1920–21, 205). Snorri (*Heimskringla* I 218–19) uses it as a proper name.

35. This sentence is now almost unreadable in the manuscript, the result of an attempt at some point to rub it out. If the reading is correct, *Ágrip* here agrees with Theodoricus (11) in claiming that Haraldr gráfeldr killed Tryggvi. In chapter XVI, where the text is quite similar to that of *Historia Norvegiæ* (110–11), it is said that 'not all tell of his [i. e. Tryggvi's] slaying in the same way'.

36. Gull-Haraldr was the son of Knútr Danaást, Haraldr blátǫnn's brother. In *Jómsvíkinga saga* (1969, 73–74; *Flateyjarbók* I 104–05) it is said that Haraldr blátǫnn was responsible for his brother Knútr's death, as he would later be for his nephew's.

37. This last speech of Haraldr gráfeldr is not found in *Heimskringla* or any of the other major Kings' Sagas, but does appear in one manuscript of *Jómsvíkinga saga* (1969, 82).

38. In the later histories Gunnhildr, as a result of all her sons proclaiming themselves king at one time or another, is referred to as *konungamóðir*, 'mother of kings'.

39. As Gunnhildr was probably Haraldr blátǫnn's sister (see note 15 above), this story—found also in Theodoricus (12–13), *Jómsvíkinga*

saga (1969, 83–84) and some manuscripts of *Óláfs saga Tryggvasonar en mesta* (I 170–71; *Flateyjarbók* I 152–53)—must be seen in the light of the medieval 'smear campaign' against Gunnhildr mentioned above (notes 15 and 17).

40. Snorri (*Heimskringla* I 295–98) calls him both Karkr and Þormóðr karkr, while he is Skopti karkr in *Jómsvíkinga saga* (1969, 185, 194) and *Fagrskinna* (139), and called just Karkr by Oddr Snorrason (1932, 78). The word itself could be related to the Norwegian (*nynorsk*) word *kark*, 'thick bark', or to *karka*, 'to tie or bind tightly' (Lind 1920–21, 189; Ásgeir Blöndal Magnússon 1989, 447).

41. Ulli is a pet-name for Erlendr (Lind 1905–15, 1056). According to Snorri (*Heimskringla* I 295) and the other sources Óláfr Tryggvason had only shortly before killed Hákon's son Erlendr, who was waiting by his father's ships.

42. Literally 'that all passages were closed'.

43. The author may here be working from two different sources, as this was already stated at the beginning of the chapter.

44. This is the only version of this story in which Karkr murders Hákon under orders, rather than on his own initiative (cf. *Heimskringla* I 297; Oddr Snorrason 1932, 83). This is perhaps meant further to demean Hákon's already inglorious death preparatory to the arrival of the spectacular figure of Óláfr Tryggvason.

45. Hákon's position had by this time so weakened that with Óláfr's return to Norway he found every hand turned against him. Although his appetite for women was legendary (cf. *Heimskringla* I 290–91), the chief reasons for his unpopularity were obviously political (see Andersen 1977, 101).

46. Karkr is said to have been hanged in most of the other sources, but in *Heimskringla* (I 298) he is beheaded.

47. *Hersir* was the traditional title of a Norwegian chieftain from the earliest times down to about the time of Haraldr hárfagri, when it came to represent a rank below *jarl*, 'earl' and above *hǫlðr*, 'yeoman, freeholder' (Fritzner 1886–96, I 804–05; see also Sogner 1961). It is highly unlikely that Hersir was ever the name of any particular king and there is no other record of any king bearing this name. Similarly, Vigða is unknown as a woman's name but does exist as a river-name (Rygh 1904, 296).

48. Sixteen verses and half-verses from the poem *Háleygjatal* (none of them relating to the incidents described here) have survived in *Heimskringla*, *Edda Snorra Sturlusonar* and *Fagrskinna* (see *Skjd*. A I 68–71; B I 60–62).

49. *Tryggvareyrr* (or *-hreyrr*, modern Tryggvarör), is the name of a large mound thought to date from the Bronze Age on the island Tryggö (ON *Tryggvaey*, 'Tryggvi's island'), to the west of Sótanes (Sotanäs). In *Historia Norvegiæ* (110) Tryggvareyrr is said to be on an island, but other sources, e. g. Oddr Snorrason (1932, 6) agree with *Ágrip* in placing it on Sótanes itself. The text seems to imply that Sótanes is in Raumaríki (Romerike), and, if so, is incorrect. It is in Ranríki (modern Bohuslän), which, according to Snorri (*Heimskringla* I 151), is where Tryggvi ruled.

50. Snorri (*Heimskringla* I 225) has Ástríðr's son born on an island in a lake after Tryggvi's death. But as it was customary for a child born after the death of its father to be named after him, that Óláfr was named after his grandfather and not his father lends credence to the story as it is related here (cf. Storm 1893, 214).

51. There is an erasure following *lúsarskegg* in which Gustav Storm was able to make out *sumir loðskeggi*, '[but] some [call] shaggy-beard' (see textual note). The reason for the erasure may be that since the author has already introduced Þórólfr in chapter IX, there calling him only *lúsaskegg* (*lúsa-* is gen. pl., *lúsar-* gen. sg.), it might have seemed odd to mention his other nickname here.

52. Sigurðr Eiríksson, Ástríðr's brother, had long been at the court of Vladimir (ON Valdamarr), son of Grand Prince Svyatoslav of Kiev. On the Kievan Rus generally see Noonan 1986 and references there.

53. The island Ösel in the Baltic (Estonian: Saaremaa).

54. The year of Óláfr's birth is usually reckoned to be 968 or 969. It is said that he was nine years old when he was ransomed by his uncle and brought to Hólmgarðr, and that he was another nine years at the court of King Vladimir (cf. *Heimskringla* I 232). This would then have been about the year 980.

55. *Gautar*, men of Gautland (modern Östergötland and Västergötland) in southern Sweden.

56. There are dozens of stories of Óláfr's exploits between the time he left Hólmgarðr (*c*.986) and his triumphant return to Norway in 994 or

995. Many are unsupported but make interesting reading. Óláfr is mentioned enough in foreign sources, however, to indicate that he was quite busy during these years. It is probable that he fought at the Battle of Maldon in 991 and with Sveinn tjúguskegg at London in 994 (see the *Anglo-Saxon Chronicle* (A, E, and F) for 993 and 994). The stories that he fought in Bornholm, lived in Wendland and plundered western Europe, however highly embellished, seem also to be based on fact; see Andersen 1977, 102–06 and references there. For summaries in English see Jones 1968b, 131–33; 1968a; Turville-Petre 1951, 133–35.

57. Jómsborg was supposed to be a town on the south Baltic coast inhabited by a group of mercenary Vikings known as the Jómsvíkingar. The principal source of information on them and their town is the early thirteenth-century *Jómsvíkinga saga*. For summaries of the debate surrounding Jómsborg and the saga's historicity see Ólafur Halldórsson's introduction to *Jómsvíkinga saga* 1969, esp. 28–51, or the introduction to Blake's edition (1962, especially vii–xv).

58. The Isles of Scilly (ON Syllingar), according to Snorri (*Heimskringla* I 266) and most of the other sources.

59. The text has here the loan word *própheti* (see note 12 above).

60. According to Snorri (*Heimskringla* I 267), Óláfr and his men were baptised then and there. A similar story is told in the 'Legendary Saga' (1982, 64) about Óláfr helgi, who is also said to have met a hermit in Britain. Both these stories may be based on the story of how Totila, Visigothic king of Italy, tested the powers of St Benedict of Nursia, which appears in the *Dialogues* of Gregory the Great, a work early translated into Norse (see Turville-Petre 1953, 135–36).

According to the *Anglo-Saxon Chronicle* for the year 994 Óláfr received baptism at Andover with King Æthelred acting as sponsor, *and him þá Anelaf behet, and eac gelæste, þæt he næfre eft to Angelcynne mid unfriðe cuman nolde.*

61. According to Icelandic sources (*Njáls saga* 256, *Kristni saga* 14, and *Óláfs saga Tryggvasonar en mesta* I 149), Þangbrandr was the son of a Saxon count named Vilbaldus. In most sources he is said to come from Bremen or Saxony. Theodoricus (15) calls him Theobrand and says that he is Flemish. Þangbrandr was the first foreign missionary to go to Iceland. He spent two or three winters there, making a few converts and many enemies, some of whom he slew (cf. *Kristni saga* 25–26; *Íslendingabók* 14). He returned to Norway in 998 or 999.

Þormóðr is also mentioned in *Kristni saga* (38), *Íslendingabók* (15) and by Oddr Snorrason (1932, 91), but no source contains any information on his origins, although he is said to have accompanied Óláfr to Norway from England.

62. *illi* ('the bad'), i. e. in contradistinction to Hákon góði.

63. His age in other sources varies from twenty-two to thirty-three, but *Ágrip*'s assertion that he was twenty-seven is in keeping with the generally accepted chronology.

64. These claims are largely exaggerated. Certainly in the more accessible areas of western Norway and the Vík most people would have been at least nominally Christian, but those in the inland districts would still have been unbaptised and pagan.

Óláfr appears to have been very persuasive. He is known to have threatened people with mutilation or death if they refused baptism. But, as we have seen already, the conversion of Norway was a process that had begun before Óláfr's return and one far from complete at the time of his death. It is not really until the death of his namesake, Óláfr helgi, that one can safely speak of a Christian Norway.

The conversion of Iceland, although in many respects untypical, is the best documented, and can serve to indicate general trends. According to Ari fróði, Christianity was accepted at the Alþingi the same summer as—in fact two or three months before—Óláfr's death. Ari also states that Óláfr had been one of the initiators of the conversion, but it cannot be said that he was wholly responsible for it. On the conversion of Norway see Andersen 1977, for Iceland Strömbäck 1975 and Hastrup 1985, 179–89, and for Scandinavia generally Sawyer 1987.

65. This was Boleslaw 'the Brave', called Búrizláfr (or -leifr) in ON, who ruled Poland from 992 to 1025 and to whom Þyri Haraldsdóttir had in fact been wedded. *Ágrip* here agrees with *Historia Norvegiæ* (116–17). The story also appears, but in a slightly different form, in *Heimskringla* (I 273, 341–43), Oddr Snorrason (1932, 143–47), and *Fagrskinna* (146–47).

66. The word *landamæri* would normally mean 'boundary', 'borderland' or 'frontier', but must logically here refer to the coast—the coast obviously also marking the extremities of the country. Margaret Ashdown (1930, 213) points to the similar use of *landgemyrce* in *Beowulf*, l. 209 (cf. Bosworth–Toller 1898, 618).

67. This was the Battle of Svǫlð(r), a favourite topic of skaldic poets and authors of Kings' Sagas. Its causes, and even its location, remain the subject of much debate (see Ellehøj 1958; or Andersen 1977, 104–05, for a summary and further references).

68. ON *rúm*, 'rooms, places': Viking ships were divided into rowing-places, one for each pair of oars. Ormr inn langi, 'the Long Serpent', was the most famous ship of the age and by all accounts one of the largest. Brøgger and Shetelig (1950, 96) state that it had places for thirty-four pairs of oars and give it an overall length of about fifty metres.

69. King Sveinn retained direct control of the Vík, the area in which Danish influence was always the greatest. King Óláfr of Sweden was given control of Ranríki in the south-east and four provinces in eastern Þrándheimr, most of which was effectively ruled by Sveinn Hákonarson as the king's vassal. Eiríkr Hákonarson ruled the western provinces of Þrándheimr and coastal provinces—in other words most of Norway—although it would be a mistake to underestimate Danish influence during this time (see Andersen 1977, 106–09).

70. 1008 was the traditional year for the death of King Sveinn, but the *Anglo-Saxon Chronicle* (E) entry for 1014 informs us that *Her on þissum geare Swegen geendode his dagas to candelmæssan .iii. Nº Febr̃.*

71. The traditional chronology takes 1012 as the year of Hákon's succession and there is no reason to doubt this; it is, however, unlikely that Eiríkr was in England before 1014. He ruled as earl in Northumbria from 1016 until his death in 1023.

72. This was Knútr inn ríki (Canute the Great) who by 1027 could in his letter to the English people title himself *Rex totius Angliae et Denemarchiae et Norregiae et partis Swavorum* (Andersen 1977, 129). He had first come to England with his father Sveinn tjúguskegg in 1013, and following Sveinn's death a year later increased his power in England until, with the death of Edmund Ironside on St Andrew's Day 1016, *feng Cnut cyng to eall Engla landes rice* (*Anglo-Saxon Chronicle* (D, under 1017)). He ruled until his death on 12 November 1035.

73. This rather unpleasant-sounding cause of death is attested by other sources (Theodoricus 25, *Fagrskinna* 167, *Óláfs saga Tryggvasonar en mesta* II 317). Snorri (*Heimskringla* II 32) says he bled to death but omits any further detail.

74. The text as it stands seems to indicate that Óláfr was called *grœnski*, i. e. from Grenland in southern Norway. Óláfr was in fact known in the early part of his life as Óláfr digri, 'the stout', and the surname *grœnski* (or *grenski*) is otherwise associated with his father Haraldr. Modern editors have therefore supplied the word *Haraldssunar*.

75. With the exception of the statement 'much is said about the extent of Óláfr's travels' at the beginning of the next chapter, *Ágrip* in fact says nothing about Óláfr's viking years; these make up on the other hand the last pages of *Historia Norvegiæ* (119–24).

76. Most of what is said about Óláfr's travels can be found in the *Víkingarvísur* (the title is modern) of Sighvatr Þórðarson (*Skjd.* A I 223–28; B I 213–16; Fell 1981). For a summary in English of Óláfr's early years based on the literary sources see Turville-Petre 1951, 140–46. Óláfr returned to Norway in the autumn of 1015, then about twenty.

77. According to Snorri and the other sources Óláfr places his two ships on either side of the strait with a thick cable tied between them, which would explain the reciprocal form 'his ships pulled towards each other' (*heimtusk saman*); cf. the 'Legendary Saga' (1982, 68), where the wording is closest to that of *Ágrip*; also *Fagrskinna* (171), *Heimskringla* (II 36–37), the Separate *Óláfs saga helga* (62–64) and Theodoricus (27).

78. There is no evidence in support of *Ágrip*'s assertion that Hákon ruled in the Hebrides.

79. Óláfr's father, Haraldr grenski, had died shortly after Óláfr was born. After his death Óláfr's mother had married Sigurðr sýr Hálfdanarson, a king in Hringaríki, part of the area known as Upplǫnd, and it was there that Óláfr grew up.

80. Óláfr had been accepted as king only by the farmers of Upplǫnd and the Vík, but Þrándheimr, home of the jarls of Hlaðir, remained loyal to Sveinn.

Nesjar was not the first meeting of Óláfr and Sveinn; they had met previously at Niðaróss, but Óláfr had not been as successful in Sveinn's territory as he was to be the following spring in his own. For the events leading up to Nesjar see Johnsen 1916; or Turville-Petre 1951, 148–50 for a summary.

81. Einarr was arguably the most important chieftain of his age and played a prominent role in Norwegian politics for over 50 years. The

meaning of his nickname, usually written *þambarskelfir*, is not entirely clear, but the possibilities are interesting enough to warrant mention here. *Þambar* is the genitive of *þǫmb*, a word meaning 'guts, belly', particularly with the notion of being blown up or extended, but which can also be used to mean 'gut-string', particularly bow-string. In view of Einarr's reputation as an archer (cf. *Heimskringla* II 27), some scholars have opted for this explanation (e. g. Lind 1920–21, 405–06). The second element, written variously *skelmir* or *skelfir*, probably means 'shaker'—although it could mean 'devil'—but whether Einarr shook his belly or his bow-string is unresolved.

82. Garðar, literally 'cities' (i. e. walled strongholds), the old Scandinavian term for the Scandinavian settlements in Russia. On the term see Pritsak 1981, esp. 217–20.

83. Yaroslav, ON Jaritláfr (or Jarizláfr, -leifr), was the son of Vladimir (see note 52 above). He ruled in Kiev from his father's death in 1016 until his own in 1054. His wife Ingigerðr died in about 1050. For the story of her betrothal to Óláfr and events following see *Heimskringla* II 114–47.

84. Gunnhildr is called Úlfhildr in *Heimskringla* (II 327–28; III 41) and elsewhere, and this is likely to be more correct as she is called Wulfhild in German sources. Otto—Ótta in *Heimskringla*—was really Ordulf (1059–72), the son of Bernhard Billung, Duke of Saxony. In contrast to the male offspring, quite a lot is known of the names and fates of Úlfhildr's descendants at least, who seem to have made out reasonably well. Ordulf and Úlfhildr had a son, Magnus (1072–1106), whose daughter—he had no male offspring—married Duke Henry the Black of Saxony and Bavaria. Their son was Henry the Proud (d. 1139), father of Henry the Lion (d. 1195), father of Otto, Duke of Brunswick Luneburg (d. 1252), from whom are descended the Hanoverians.

85. This is also mentioned by Guillaume de Jumièges (1914, 81–82) and Adam of Bremen (1917, 112), and in *Historia Norvegiæ* (121–22), but not, for example, by Theodoricus or Snorri.

86. The battle between Óláfr and Erlingr was fought on 21 December 1028 at the island of Bokn, near Tungunes in Jaðarr (modern Jæren).

87. According to Snorri (*Heimskringla* II 192) Áslákr and Erlingr were kinsmen.

88. Legally, *níðingr* designated a person who had committed a crime which could not be atoned for, and who could therefore be killed with impunity. The term carried with it a sense of 'unmanliness' (if one takes manliness in the sense of 'all that may become a man'), hence its use here of a traitor; treason was unmanly (see Sørensen 1980, esp. 16–39; 1983, 14–32).

89. According to Theodoricus (31) and Snorri (*Heimskringla* II 335) Hákon Eiríksson drowned in the Pentland Firth (see Stenton 1971, 405).

Sveinn was Knútr's son by his English consort Ælfgyfu (ON Álfífa), daughter of Ælfhelm, aldorman of Northampton. This was 'the other Ælfgyfu', not Ælfgyfu, or Emma as she was more commonly called, Æthelred's widow, whom Knútr married in 1017. See Stenton 1971, 397, and the *Anglo-Saxon Chronicle* II 211.

90. *Vinartoddi*: *vinar*, more correctly *vinjar*, is the genitive of *vin*, 'meadow', a word occuring otherwise only in proper names, while *toddi* is a 'bit' or 'piece' (Fritzner 1886–96, III 949; 709), and the meaning of the whole is therefore 'a bit of the meadow', a part of the farmer's yearly produce paid as tax to the king.

91. *Rygjartó*: *rygjar* is from *rygr*, 'lady', and *tó* means 'unspun wool or flax' (Fritzner 1886–96, III 141; 709). These terms can also be found in medieval Norwegian law books such as the *Frostaþingslǫg* (*NgL* I 257–58). The close similarity between *Ágrip* and the texts of the laws themselves suggests that the author was either working from a legal text or was at least familiar with legal terminology (*Ágrip* 1984, xiii; Andersen 1977, 138).

92. In Norway the unit for the organisation of the levy or conscription was the *hamla* (pl. *hǫmlur*), this being the loop into which the oar was fitted, representing a single oarsman.

93. The text here has *hérlenzkr ok útlenzkr*, literally 'here-landish and out-landish'; Snorri, writing in Iceland, has in the corresponding passage in *Heimskringla* (II 400) *þarlenzkr ok útlenzkr*, 'there-landish and out-landish'.

94. Cf. chapter LII below.

95. The traditional date for the Battle of Stiklastaðir (or in some sources Stiklarstaðir; modern Stiklestad) was 29 July 1030; see Andersen 1977, 132–33.

96. Haraldr, later called harðráði ('hard-ruler'), was Óláfr's half-brother, son of Sigurðr sýr ('sow') and Ásta Guðbrandsdóttir. Rǫgnvaldr Brúsason was jarl of Orkney (d. 1045). Bjǫrn digri was Óláfr's marshal.

97. Sighvatr Þórðarson was an Icelander who came to King Óláfr's court in about 1015. The verse cited here can also be found in the 'Legendary Saga' (1982, 208; see also *Skjd.* A I 274; B I 253).

98. This date, the only attempt at absolute chronology in *Ágrip*, derives from Theodoricus (42): *occubuit autem beatus Olavus . . . anno ab incarnatione Domini millesimo vicesimo nono, ut nos certius indagare potuimus* (i. e. 'as far as we can tell'). Bjarni Einarsson (*Ágrip* 1984, xxxvi) suggests that this was Theodoricus's attempt to reconcile the year 1028, found in *Acta Sancti Olavi regis et martyris* (131–32), and the year 1030, given by Ari fróði and all later Icelandic historians as well as by the *Anglo-Saxon Chronicle* (E). Interestingly, Theodoricus begins his next chapter with the observation *Sciendum vero est, in libris nil adeo corruptum ut supputationen numerorum.* It should also be noted that *Ágrip*'s own (relative) chronology, reckoning from the fall of Óláfr helgi to the Battle of Stamford Bridge (nineteen days before Hastings), would have the Normans invade England in 1065 (see *Ágrip* 1984, lix).

99. If by this it is meant that Haraldr claimed the kingship immediately after Óláfr's death it is the only one of the sources to say so. If this is not what is meant, it is not clear what is.

100. Miracles attributed to Óláfr are said to have been reported within hours of his death at Stiklastaðir. Óláfr's body was exhumed—according to some sources it rose to the surface of its own accord—a year and five days after his death and was found to be uncorrupted (see the 'Legendary Saga' 1982, especially 220–36; also Turville-Petre 1951, 159–64; Jones 1968a).

101. What his contemporaries viewed as the 'harshness' of Magnús's first years of rule, a theme in the skaldic poetry of the time (e. g. Sighvatr's *Bersǫglisvísur* and Arnórr Þórðarson's *Hrynhenda*), was probably his taking revenge on his father's former opponents and his continuation of the taxation policies instituted by Sveinn and Álfífa (Andersen 1977, 144).

102. This is one of nine strophes cited by Snorri (*Heimskringla* III 26–30), one of thirteen in the manuscript known as *Hulda* (fol. 4) and

one of sixteen in *Flateyjarbók* (III 267–69). The poem as a whole is known as *Bersǫglisvísur* (or *-flokkur*), 'the plain-speaking verses' (*Skjd*. A I 251–56; B I 234–39).

103. Hǫrða-Knútr, from Hǫrð in Jutland, was Knútr's son by Emma of Normandy, and therefore his only legitimate heir. For an exhaustive discussion of the name, see Campbell 1949, 97–98.

104. Some historians have denied the existence of this agreement, but the anonymous *Chronicon Roskildense* (*SmhDmæ*. I 22), written *c*.1140, agrees with *Ágrip* on this point (Andersen 1977, 161–62).

105. The *Anglo-Saxon Chronicle* (C) for the year 1042 reports:

> Hér gefor Harðacnut swa þæt he æt his drince stód. Ond he færinga feoll to þære eorðan mid egeslicum anginne, ond hine gelæhton ðe þar neh wæron, ond he syððan nan word ne gecwæð. Ond he forðferde on vi Iđ Iun.

106. Sveinn is commonly known as Estridsson (Estrid being the Danish form of Ástríðr). Ástríðr/Estrid was the daughter of Sveinn tjúguskegg, and Knútr's half-sister and also the half-sister of King Óláfr the Swede. Sveinn grew up in Sweden and went to England probably in the year 1039. Ágrip is the only source of information on Sveinn's stay in England. After Magnús's death Sveinn ruled Denmark until his own death in 1074.

107. According to Snorri (*Heimskringla* III 56) the battle of Helganes was fought a full year after the Battle of Hlýrskógsheiðr. Sveinn and Magnús first met in the autumn of 1042, shortly after Magnús had been received as king. Their meeting at Gautelfr (modern Göta älv) was peaceful, ending with their pledges of friendship and allegiance. Sveinn was made *jarl*, to rule over Denmark as king's regent as his father Úlfr Þorgilsson had done before him.

108. Hlýrskógsheiðr (Lyrskovshede) lies in fact about 100 km to the south of Skotborgará (now Kongeå), to the northwest of Hedeby in Schleswig.

109. Haraldr came to Sweden in 1045 and to Norway the following year. Snorri's *Haralds saga Sigurðarsonar* (*Heimskringla* III 68–90) provides a fictionalised account of Haraldr's exploits after Stiklastaðir as a member of the famous Varangian guard in Constantinople. Sigfús Blöndal (1954, 108–68; 1978, 54–102) examines all the written sources pertaining to Haraldr.

110. Úlfr stalleri was an Icelander, the nephew of Guðrún Ósvífrsdóttir of *Laxdœla saga*. According to Snorri (*Heimskringla* III 79) he had been with Haraldr in the Varangian guard, which only underlines the unlikelihood of this story. Úlfr was King Haraldr's marshal, not Magnús's.

111. A less joyful meeting is described by Snorri (*Heimskringla* III 94–102).

112. *Heikilnef* is a *hapax legomenon* of uncertain meaning; Lind 1920–21, 140, suggests 'snippnäsa' (i. e. 'pointy-nosed'; cf. Ásgeir Blöndal Magnússon 1989, 314).

113. Magnús died on 25 October 1047.

114. This sentence bears a striking resemblance to the 39th verse of *Nóregskonungatal* (*Flateyjarbók* II 524), leading some to conclude that it derives from Sæmundr's lost book (Ellehøj 1965, 264; see Introduction p. xvi).

115. Ragnhildr, who later married Hákon Ívarsson, the great-grandson of Hákon Sigurðarson.

116. Þóra, daughter of Þórbergr Árnason. His brother Finnr (Fiðr) was married to Bergljót Hálfdanardóttir, King Haraldr's niece. Kálfr Árnason, mentioned above (chapters XXVI and XXXI) was another of the brothers. Haraldr was already married to Ellisif (Elizabeth), the daughter of Jaroslav and Ingigerðr Óláfsdóttir and it is therefore more likely that Þóra was his mistress than his queen; it was their issue, however, Magnús and Óláfr, that became the more prominent. According to the text here, Finnr lived *austr í Ranríki*, 'east in Ranríki'. This is probably a mistake in the text, however, as according to Snorri (*Heimskringla* III 126) Finnr Árnason lived *á Yrjum á Austrátt*, i. e. on the farm Austrátt (moden Austrått) in the area Yrjar, on the northern side of the mouth of the Trondheim Fjord. It is not difficult to imagine a copyist misreading an exemplar which read *á Austrátt á Yrjum*, particularly as *austrátt* can also mean 'easterly direction'.

117. Snorri bases their quarrel on more complicated yet equally personal grounds (see *Heimskringla* III 126–35).

118. Halland is in southwestern Sweden, but at this time was politically part of Denmark. Haraldr of Norway and Sveinn of Denmark met in battle at the mouth of the River Niz on 9 August 1062.

119. *mœddr við eld*: literally 'exhausted with fire'. This story is not found in *Heimskringla*, but is recorded in *Morkinskinna*, 204–05.

120. Tostig (ON Tósti) was Harold's younger brother. He had been made Earl of Northumbria in 1055, but was expelled from England along with his family and retainers following a revolt in Northumbria for which it seems he was partially to blame (Stenton 1971, 578–79).

121. *Sjaldan fór svá, þá er vel vildi*. Theodoricus has *Raro . . . tale signum portendit victoriam* (57). Snorri (*Heimskringla* III 186) also relates the incident, but has the king more optimistically say *Fall er fararheill*, 'a fall is a good omen for a journey'. In *Sverris saga* (1920, 35) Jarl Erlingr says: *Eigi fór þá svá er vel vildi*.

122. Óláfr Haraldsson is called *bóndi* (older form *búandi*), 'farmer', in *Ágrip* and a few other sources (e. g. *Heimskringla* III 208), but is more commonly known as Óláfr kyrri, 'the quiet' or 'the peaceful' (see Lind 1920–21, 36; 231).

123. Elgjusetr (modern Elgeseter, near Trondheim) was an Augustinian monastery founded probably by Archbishop Eysteinn Erlendsson in about 1170.

124. This was to become the great cathedral of Kristskirkja (modern Kristkirken), though it was certainly not completed during Óláfr's lifetime (see *Heimskringla* III 204).

125. Miklagildi: 'the Great Guild'; each guild had a patron saint and the guildsmen would meet on the saint's feast day (see Blom 1960). St Óláfr was the patron saint of Miklagildi; his feast day was 29 July, the day of the Battle of Stiklastaðir (see *Heimskringla* III 204–05).

126. This half-strophe is found also in *Heimskringla* in the last chapter of Snorri's *Haralds saga Sigurðarsonar* (*Heimskringla* III 202) and in *Morkinskinna* (292). Its author is unknown.

127. Only *Ágrip* calls him *berleggr*, 'bare-leg'; in *Heimskringla* and all other sources he is known as Magnús berfœtr or berbeinn, the meaning of which is the same (Lind 1920–21, 21). Snorri explains that Magnús was called by this name because after returning from 'west viking' he and his men dressed 'as was the custom in the western lands [i. e. the British Isles]' and describes what are clearly meant to be kilts. Bjarni Aðalbjarnarson (*Heimskringla* III 229) points out that nowhere in Snorri's source material is Magnús's nickname explained; it is not known whether kilt-wearing was in fact a custom in Ireland in Magnús's day, and it is not unlikely that Snorri's explanation is merely the one that seemed most likely to him. Cf. also *Ágrip*, chapter

LI: 'he wore gaiters (*stighosur*), as was his custom.' For an alternative explanation of his nickname see Saxo Grammaticus 1931, 342.

128. Skúlagarðr was the old kings' residence, named after the English Skúli, foster-father of Óláfr kyrri (see *Heimskringla* III 197).

129. Klémetskirkja (Klemenskirken) is the oldest church in Trondheim, built by Óláfr Tryggvason.

130. Hefring (Høvringen): a headland to the west of Trondheim.

131. Dofrafjall (Dovrefjell) according to Snorri (*Heimskringla* III 212).

132. Sveinn was a Dane according to Snorri (*Heimskringla* III 213).

133. Vagnvíkastrǫnd (now Leksvikstrand) is immediately across the fjord from Trondheim. The name *Vagnvík* survives in Vanvikan, the bay at the western end of Leksvikstrand.

134. According to Snorri (*Heimskringla* III 213), Þórir was *gamall maðr ok þungfœrr* ('an old man and slow-going'), and, in his own words, as Snorri reports them (III 216), *heill at hǫndum, en hrumr at fótum*, 'hale of hand but feeble of foot' (also in *Fagrskinna* 304).

135. This verse also appears in the other major vernacular Kings' Sagas, *Heimskringla* (III 216), *Morkinskinna* (304), and *Fagrskinna* (305); see also *Skjd.* A I 434, B I 403. Perkins (1987) relates it to Old Norse rowing chants and children's verses.

136. Snorri (*Heimskringla* III 217) says of this statement that *í því sýndisk, at konungr vildi hafa verit beðinn, at Egill hefði lifat* ('from this it was evident that the king had wanted to be asked to spare Egill's life'). Little is known of Egill's family—in *Heimskringla* he is called Ásláksson, Áskelsson here—but his wife Ingibjǫrg's family was among the most prominent in Norway and Magnús might have expected them to come forward on Egill's behalf. This would account for the references to Egill's wife and her family here. But by 'kin' (*frændr*) Magnús could also be referring to himself: his grandmother Þóra Þorbergsdóttir was Ǫgmundr's sister, aunt of Egill's wife Ingibjǫrg.

137. *Skutilsveinn* was a title of honour derived from the ON *skutill*, 'a plate or small table' (from OE *scutel*, Lat. *scutella*). Those with this title were involved with the everyday running of the king's household (see Hamre 1971).

138. Ingi Steinkelsson, who ruled Sweden c.1080–1110.

139. According to Theodoricus (61–62) there were two separate attacks, the second of which ended in defeat for Magnús. *Morkinskinna* (324, 328) similarly records two battles against Ingi at Fuxerna; Magnús is said to have been victorious in the first, while the outcome of the second is not explicitly stated. In *Fagrskinna* (310–11) and *Heimskringla* (III 226–28) there are two campaigns to Sweden, but only one battle against Ingi, indecisive in *Fagrskinna* but a defeat for Magnús in *Heimskringla*.

140. These figures, and those mentioned in the previous sentence, were all prominent in eleventh-century Norwegian politics.

141. St Magnús of Orkney (d. 1116).

142. Hugi digri ('the stout') was Hugh, son of Richard, Viscount of Avranches, whom King William made Earl of Chester in 1101. This account is found also in Theodoricus (62), but according to Snorri (*Heimskringla* III 222), *Morkinskinna* (319) and other sources it was another earl, Hugi prúði ('the magnificent')—Hugh of Montgomery, Earl of Shrewsbury—whom Magnús killed. See A. Bugge 1914, 38–40; Charles 1934, 116–22.

143. Irish annals indicate that Magnús was in Ireland by 1102, when he conquered Dublin and made a pact with Muirchertach (ON Mýrjartak, or in some sources Mýrkjartan) Úa Briain (1086–1119), King of Munster, arranging for the marriage of his son Sigurðr (then either nine or twelve depending on the source) and Muirchertach's daughter, said to have been five years old at the time. Magnús spent the winter on Man, and the following summer joined with Muirchertach in an attack on Domnall Úa Lochlainn, a king in Ulster. They were badly defeated in battle on 5 August, and according to Snorri (*Heimskringla* III 234–37) were awaiting supplies from Muirchertach in order to return to Norway when they were attacked by a large army of Irishmen. Irish annals relate that Magnús was killed by Ulstermen while raiding there, in County Down, in 1103. See A. Bugge 1914, 30–49; Ó Corráin 1972, 142–50.

144. *Morkinskinna* (334) follows *Ágrip* in this, but in *Heimskringla* (III 234) Magnús is said to have died on Bartholomew's Day itself (24 August).

145. Called Eyvindr ǫlbogi, 'elbow', in *Heimskringla* (III 233) and there said to be the king's marshal (*stallari*).

146. In *Heimskringla* (III 224) Mýrjartak is said to be the son of King Þjálbi rather than Kondjálfi, which may be a scribal error, i. e. *konungs Þjálbasonar* for *Kondjálfasonar*. He was in fact Muirchertach, son of Toirdelbach Úa Briain, grandson of Brian Bóroimhe. His daughter Biadmuin married Magnús's son Sigurðr in 1102. Magnús set Sigurðr over Man, but he ruled it possibly less than a year before his father's death brought him back to Norway. In *Fagrskinna* (315) it is said that Sigurðr left her *fyrir vestan haf . . . ok vildi þá ekki eiga hana*, 'in the west . . . and did not want to be married to her' (cf. *Morkinskinna* 337).

147. Cf. chapter XXIX. Snorri does not mention that the brothers abolished these laws till after his account of Sigurðr's return from Jerusalem (*Heimskringla* III 256).

148. Sigurðr left Norway in 1107 or 1108 and arrived in Palestine in 1110. See Runciman 1951–54, II 92–93, on how Sigurðr helped the Franks besiege Sidon.

149. *Við landsenda*: this was at Konungahella, on the northern side of the Göta älv. The church was called Krosskirkja.

150. An army of heathen Wends attacked Konungahella in 1135. The *Annales regii* or *Konungsannáll* (Storm 1888, 113) for that year notes succinctly: *Undr í Konungahellu*, 'miracle at Konungahella'; cf. *Heimskringla* III 288–96.

151. There is a leaf missing from the manuscript at this point, but the text of *Morkinskinna* (352–53) gives a fair idea of what followed.

152. The text that preceded these lines can be reconstructed from chapter XXIV of *Magnússona saga* in *Heimskringla* (III 263–64). Sigurðr Jórsalafari and the Danish king Níkolás had agreed to meet in Eyrarsund (Øresund), their intention being to Christianise the people of Smálǫnd (Småland). The Danes arrived first and, growing tired of waiting, decided to return home. This angered Sigurðr, who in retaliation decided to raid Danish possessions in the area, taking the town Tumaþorp (modern Östra Tommarp). They then went on into Sweden and plundered the market town Kalmarnar (Kalmar) and other parts of Smálǫnd.

153. There was an eclipse of the sun, total in the vicinity of Þrándheimr, on 11 August 1124.

154. *Óhœgyndi*, 'discomfort'; Sigurðr was subject to fits of madness, called by Snorri *staðleysi*, 'restlessness', or perhaps 'instability, lack of self-control', an example of which he provides in *Magnússona saga* (*Heimskringla* III 262).

155. Magnús was born in 1115, Sigurðr's son by Borghildr Óláfsdóttir (*Heimskringla* III 257–58).

156. From Irish *gille-Críst*, 'servant of Christ'. Haraldr is more commonly referred to as *gilli*. On Haraldr and the events following his arrival in Norway see Helle 1974, 24–27.

157. In other words he offered to submit to ordeal. Ordeal was often resorted to in cases such as this where proof could be offered in no other way. The most common form of ordeal was *járnburðr*, which involved carrying red-hot iron, but walking over iron was not unknown. The ordeal normally took place on a Wednesday; the hands and feet were immediately bandaged and inspected on the following Saturday. If the wound was clean the man was innocent of the crime of which he had been accused or the truth of his assertion was granted. If not the man was judged guilty or accounted a liar. The ordeal was unknown in Norway before Christian times and seems to have been introduced from England by missionaries. Ordeals were always conducted under the auspices of the Church. The practice was banned in 1247 (see Hamre 1960).

158. Sæheimr is the modern Sem in Jarlsberg, Vestfold. (It is clearly a different place from the Sæheimr mentioned in ch. VI, which was in Norðhǫrðaland.)

159. There is a lacuna here of four leaves, the contents of which have been much discussed. It is unlikely that it contained anything not found in Snorri's *Magnúss saga blinda ok Haralds gilla* (*Heimskringla* III 278–302). *Ágrip* resumes at about the same point as Snorri begins chapter XXI of his *Haraldssona saga* (*Heimskringla* III 330). This was the beginning of a period of unrest that lasted until the rise to power of King Sverrir (see Helle 1974, 20–47; Gathorne-Hardy 1956).

160. Ingi, Sigurðr and Eysteinn were the three eldest sons (by three different women) of Haraldr gilli.

161. In the manuscript there is a space at the beginning of the list of names, before *ok Ǫmundi*, where a word of about nine letters has been erased. Snorri lists the same men in the same order, but names first one

Sáða-Gyrðr (which Storm claimed to be able to make out here). Sáða-Gyrðr Bárðarson (not the Gyrðr mentioned later in this chapter) was the foster-father of Sigurðr Haraldsson.

Erlingr skakki was so called because he held his head at an angle as the result of a battle-wound. He and Qgmundr dengir were in fact half-brothers. In *Morkinskinna* and *Heimskringla* the comment that Qgmundr was 'the one who achieved by far the greater honour while they both lived' is put the other way round, i. e. that *lítils þótti vert um Erling, meðan Qgmundr lifði*, 'little was thought of Erlingr while Qgmundr lived' (*Heimskringla* III 330; cf. *Morkinskinna* 445). Erlingr later married the daughter of Sigurðr Jórsalafari and became the effective ruler of Norway after twenty years of chaos during which the sons of Haraldr gilli had fought among themselves. He was eventually slain by Sverrir Sigurðarson in 1179.

162. According to Saxo Grammaticus (1931, 446–47), Ingi had been dropped by his nurse in infancy and was crippled as a result:

> Sed infantiæ suæ tempore per incuriam nutricis forte sinu delapsus, ita humo inflictus est, ut, confracto dorso, reliquum vitæ tempus gibbo oneratus exigeret. In quo quidem homine excellentis animi venustatem corporis deformitate affecti ludibrio fœdatam putares neque discernere queas, maius fortunæ beneficium receperit an opprobrium senserit.'

163. This story is absent from *Heimskringla* and *Fagrskinna* but appears in *Morkinskinna* (448–53). The text of the story in *Morkinskinna* is on the whole fuller and would appear to be more original than that preserved here (*Ágrip* 1984, xliii–xliv). The episode centres around Gregóríús Dagsson, who has not yet been introduced into the story as it is preserved in *Ágrip* although his name was mentioned in chapter L. Gregóríús was the son of Dagr Eilífsson, who is said in the story to be married to Ragnhildr, the sister of Gyða. After killing Gersteinn, Gyrðr flees, seeking shelter with Gregóríús, who protects him from Gersteinn's sons, when they come seeking revenge, and kills them both. For this Gregóríús incurs the wrath of King Sigurðr munnr, which leads ultimately to his becoming King Ingi's counsellor and general.

BIBLIOGRAPHY AND ABBREVIATIONS

Acta Sancti Olavi regis et martyris. In *MHN* 125–44.

Adam of Bremen. 1917. *Gesta Hammaburgensis ecclesiae pontificum*. Ed. Bernhard Schmeidler.

Ágrip 1834 = 'Brudstykke af en gammel norsk Kongesaga'. Ed. P. A. Munch. In *Samlinger til det norske Folks Sprog og Historie* II, 273–335.

Ágrip 1835 = 'Stutt ágrip af Noregs konúnga sögum'. Ed. Finnur Magnússon. In *Fornmanna sögur* X, 377–421.

Ágrip 1836 = 'Kort Omrids af de norske Kongers Sagaer'. Trans. N. M. Petersen. In *Oldnordiske Sagaer* X, 329–71.

Ágrip 1841 = 'Epitome historiarum regum Norvegicorum'. Trans. Sveinbjörn Egilsson. In *Scripta historica Islandorum* X, 350–92.

Ágrip 1880 = *Ágrip af Noregs konunga sögum*. Ed. Verner Dahlerup.

Ágrip 1929 = *Ágrip af Nóregs konunga sǫgum*. Ed. Finnur Jónsson. Altnordische Saga-Bibliothek XVIII.

Ágrip 1936 = *Ågrip: Ei liti norsk kongesoge*. Ed. Gustav Indrebø. Norrøne bokverk XXXII.

Ágrip 1984 = *Ágrip af Nóregskonunga sǫgum*. Ed. Bjarni Einarsson. ÍF XXIX.

Alexander Jóhannesson. 1923–24. *Íslenzk tunga í fornöld*.

Andersen, Per Sveaas. 1977. *Samlingen av Norge og kristningen av landet 800–1130*.

Andersson, Theodore M. 1979. 'Ari's *Konunga Ævi* and the Earliest Accounts of Hákon Jarl's Death.' In *Opuscula* VI. Bibliotheca Arnamagnæana XXXIII, 1–17.

Andersson, Theodore M. 1985. 'Kings' Sagas (*Konungasögur*)'. In *Old Norse–Icelandic Literature: A Critical Guide*. Ed. Carol Clover and John Lindow. Islandica XLV, 197–238.

Anglo-Saxon Chronicle = *Two of the Saxon Chronicles Parallel* I–II. 1892–99. Ed. Charles Plummer.

Árni Björnsson. 1990. 'Tímatal'. In *Alþýðuvísindi*. Ed. Frosti F. Jóhannesson. Íslensk þjóðmenning VII, 51–101.

Ásgeir Blöndal Magnússon. 1989. *Íslensk orðsifjabók*.

Ashdown, Margaret. 1930. *English and Norse Documents relating to the Reign of Ethelred the Unready*.

Bandle, Oskar. 1956. *Die Sprache der Guðbrandsbiblía*. Bibliotheca Arnamagnæana XVII.

Beyschlag, Siegfried. 1950. *Konungasögur: Untersuchungen zur Königssaga bis Snorri: Die Älteren Übersichtswerke samt Ynglingasaga*. Bibliotheca Arnamagnæana VIII.

Bjarni Aðalbjarnarson. 1937. *Om de norske kongers sagaer*.
Bjarni Guðnason. 1977. 'Theodoricus og íslenskir sagnaritarar'. In *Sjötíu ritgerðir helgaðar Jakobi Benediktssyni*. Ed. Einar G. Pétursson and Jónas Kristjánsson, 107–120.
Blom, Grethe Authén. 1960. 'Gilde. Norge'. In *KLNM*, V 308–13.
Blöndal, Sigfús. 1954. *Væringjasaga*. English translation by Benedikt S. Benedikz, *The Varangians of Byzantium*, 1978.
Bosworth–Toller 1898 = *An Anglo-Saxon Dictionary based on the manuscript collections of the late Joseph Bosworth*. Ed. T. N. Toller.
Brieskorn, Roland. 1909. 'Isländska handskriftsstudier', *Arkiv för nordisk filologi* XXV, 147–78.
Brøgger, A. W. and Shetelig, Haakon. 1950. *Vikingeskipene: deres forgjengere og etterfølgere*. English translation by Katherine John, *The Viking Ships: Their Ancestry and Evolution*, 1951.
Bugge, Alexander. 1914. *Smaa bidrag til Norges historie paa 1000-tallet*.
Bugge, Sophus. 1873. 'Bemærkninger om den i Skotland fundne latinske Norges Krønike', *Aarbøger for nordisk Oldkyndighed og Historie*, 1–49.
Campbell, Alistair. 1949, repr. 1998. *Encomium Emmae reginae*.
Cederschiöld, Gustaf. 1884. *Fornsögur Suðrlanda*.
Charles, B. G. 1934. *Old Norse Relations with Wales*.
Chesnutt, Michael. 1985. 'The Dalhousie Manuscript of the *Historia Norvegiae*'. In *Opuscula* VIII. Bibliotheca Arnamagnæana XXXVIII, 54–95.
Cleasby–Vigfússon 1957 = *An Icelandic–English Dictionary*. Initiated by Richard Cleasby, subsequently revised, enlarged and completed by Gudbrand Vigfusson. 2nd ed. by William A. Craigie.
Dalberg, Vibeke and Sørensen, John Kousgård. 1972–79. *Stednavneforskning* I–II.
Edda Snorra Sturlusonar I–III. 1848–87. Ed. Jón Sigurðsson *et al.*
Edda Snorra Sturlusonar. 1931. Ed. Finnur Jónsson.
Egils saga = *Egils saga Skalla-Grímssonar*. 1933. Ed. Sigurður Nordal. ÍF II.
Ellehøj, Svend. 1958. 'The location of the fall of Olaf Tryggvason'. In *Þriðji Víkingafundur. Third Viking Congress, Reykjavík 1956*. Árbók Hins íslenzka fornleifafélags, Fylgirit, 63–73.
Ellehøj, Svend. 1965. *Studier over den ældste norrøne historieskrivning*. Bibliotheca Arnamagnæana XXVI.
Fagrskinna. In *Ágrip af Nóregskonunga sǫgum. Fagrskinna—Nóregs konunga tal*. 1984. Ed. Bjarni Einarsson. ÍF XXIX.
Fell, Christine. 1981. 'Víkingarvísur'. In *Speculum norroenum: Norse Studies in Memory of Gabriel Turville-Petre*. Ed. Ursula Dronke *et al.*, 106–22.

Finnur Jónsson. 1920–24. *Den oldnorske og oldislandske litteraturs historie* I–III. 2nd ed.

Finnur Jónsson. 1928. 'Ágrip', *Aarbøger for nordisk Oldkyndighed og Historie*, 261–317.

Flateyjarbók = *Flateyjarbok: En samling af norske Konge-Sagaer med indskudte mindre Fortællinger om Begivenheder i og udenfor Norge samt Annaler* I–III. 1860–68. Ed. Guðbrandur Vigfússon and C. R. Unger.

Fritzner, Johan. 1886–96. *Ordbog over det gamle norske Sprog* I–III.

Gathorne-Hardy, G. M. 1956. *A Royal Impostor: King Sverre of Norway.*

Gjessing, A. 1873–76. *Undersøgelse af Kongesagaens Fremvæxt* I–II.

Grettis saga. In *Grettis saga Ásmundarsonar. Bandamanna saga. Odds þáttr Ófeigssonar.* 1936. Ed. Guðni Jónsson. ÍF VII.

Guðbrandur Vigfússon. 1878. 'Prolegomena'. In *Sturlunga saga* I, xvii–ccxiv.

Guillaume de Jumièges. 1914. *Gesta Normannorum Ducum.* Ed. J. Marx.

Hagland, Jan Ragnar. 1989. 'Hasleyjarsund eller Haugasund? Litt namnehistorie frå indre hamnestrok i sildabyen', *Namn og nemne* VI, 7–14.

Halvorsen, Eyvind Fjeld. 1962. 'Høvisk stil'. In *KLNM*, VII 315–18.

Hamre, Lars. 1960. 'Gudsdom: Norge'. In *KLNM*, V 551–53.

Hamre, Lars. 1971. 'Skutilsveinn'. In *KLNM*, XVI 35–36.

Hanssen, Jens S. Th. 1949. *Omkring Historia Norwegiae.*

Hastrup, Kirsten. 1985. *Culture and History in Medieval Iceland.*

Heimskringla I–III = Snorri Sturluson. 1941–51. *Heimskringla.* Ed. Bjarni Aðalbjarnarson. ÍF XXVI–XXVIII.

Helle, Knut. 1974. *Norge blir en stat 1130–1319.*

Historia Norvegiæ. In *MHN* 69–124.

Historia Regum Britanniae 1985–88 = *The Historia Regum Britannie of Geoffrey of Monmouth* I–II. Ed. Neil Wright.

Hreinn Benediktsson. 1962. 'The Unstressed and the Non-Syllabic Vowels of Old Icelandic', *Arkiv för nordisk filologi* LXXVII, 7–31.

Hreinn Benediktsson. 1965. *Early Icelandic Script as Illustrated in Vernacular Texts from the Twelfth to the Thirteenth Centuries.*

Hulda = *Hulda. Sagas of the Kings of Norway 1035–1177: Manuscript No. 66 fol. in the Arnamagnæan Collection.* 1968. Ed. Jonna Louis-Jensen. Early Icelandic Manuscripts in Facsimile VIII.

Hægstad, Marius. 1906–42. *Vestnorske maalføre fyre 1350.* 7 vols.

Hødnebø, Finn. 1974. 'Tilnavne: Norge og Island'. In *KLNM*, XVIII 318–21.

ÍF = *Íslenzk fornrit* 1933– .

Indrebø, Gustav. 1922. 'Aagrip', *Edda* XVII, 18–65.
Indrebø, Gustav. 1938–39. 'Nokre merkader til den norröne kongesoga', *Arkiv för nordisk filologi* LIV, 58–79.
Indrebø, Gustav. 1940. 'Ágrip—Hryggjarstykki', *Arkiv för nordisk filologi* LV, 342.
Íslendingabók. In *Íslendingabók. Landnámabók*. 1968. Ed. Jakob Benediktsson. ÍF I.
Johannisson, Ture. 1939. *Verbal och postverbal partikelkomposition i de germanska språken*.
Johnsen, Oscar Albert. 1916. *Olav Haraldssons ungdom indtil slaget ved Nesjar 25. mars 1016: En kritisk undersøkelse*.
Jómsvíkinga saga 1962 = *The Saga of the Jomsvikings*. Ed. N. F. Blake.
Jómsvíkinga saga. 1969. Ed. Ólafur Halldórsson.
Jón Helgason. 1934. 'Introduction'. In *Morkinskinna: MS. No. 1009 fol. in the Old Royal Collection of the Royal Library, Copenhagen*. Corpus Codicum Islandicorum Medii Aevi VI.
Jón Jóhannesson. 1956. *Íslendinga saga* I. *Þjóðveldisöld*. English translation by Haraldur Bessason, *A History of the Old Icelandic Commonwealth*, 1974.
Jón Aðalsteinn Jónsson. 1959. 'Ágrip af sögu íslenzkrar stafsetningar', *Íslenzk tunga* I, 71–119.
Jón Þorkelsson. 1856. 'Um Fagrskinnu og Ólafs sögu helga'. In *Safn til sögu Íslands og íslenzkra bókmenta* I, 137–84.
Jónas Kristjánsson. 1972. *Um Fóstbræðrasögu*.
Jónas Kristjánsson. 1981. 'Learned Style or Saga Style?' In *Speculum norroenum: Norse Studies in Memory of Gabriel Turville-Petre*. Ed. Ursula Dronke *et al.*, 260–92.
Jones, Gwyn. 1968a. *The Legendary History of Olaf Tryggvason*. The W. P. Ker Memorial Lectures XXII.
Jones, Gwyn. 1968b. *A History of the Vikings*.
Katalog 1889–94 = Kålund, Kr. *Katalog over den arnamagnæanske Håndskriftsamling* I–II.
Kjartan G. Ottósson. 1992. *The Icelandic Middle Voice: The Morphological and Phonological Development*.
KLNM = *Kulturhistorisk leksikon for nordisk middelalder* I–XXII. 1956–78. [References are to column nos.]
Koht, Halvdan. 1919. 'Den fyrste norske nasjonalhistoria', *Edda* XII, 90–118.
Koht, Halvdan. 1921. *Innhogg og utsyn i norsk historie*.
Konráð Gíslason. 1846. *Um frum-parta íslenzkrar túngu í fornöld*.

Kristni saga. In *Kristnisaga*. *Þáttr Þorvalds en víðfǫrla*. *Þáttr Ísleifs biskups Gizurarsonar*. *Hungrvaka*. 1905. Ed. B. Kahle. Altnordische Saga-Bibliothek XI.

Landnámabók. In *Íslendingabók*. *Landnámabók*. 1968. Ed. Jakob Benediktsson. ÍF I.

Lange, Gudrun. 1989. *Die Anfänge der isländisch–norwegischen Geschichtsschreibung*. Studia Islandica XLVII.

'Legendary Saga' 1922 = *Olafs saga hins helga: Efter pergamenthaandskrift i Uppsala Universitetsbibliotek, Delagardieske samling nr. 8^{II}*. Ed. Oscar Albert Johnsen.

'Legendary Saga' 1982 = *Olafs saga hins helga: Die 'Legendarische Saga' über Olaf den Heiligen (Hs. Delagard. saml. nr. 8^{II})*. Ed. Anne Heinrichs, Doris Janssen, Elke Radicke and Hartmut Röhn.

Lexicon Poeticum = Sveinbjörn Egilsson. 1931. *Lexicon poeticum antiquæ linguæ septentrionalis*. 2nd edition revised by Finnur Jónsson.

Lind, E. H. 1905–15. *Norsk–isländska dopnamn ock fingerade namn från medeltiden*. [References are to column numbers.]

Lind, E. H. 1920–21. *Norsk–isländska personbinamn från medeltiden*. [References are to column numbers.]

Lorenz, Gottfried (ed.). 1984. Snorri Sturluson. *Gylfaginning*.

Maurer, Konrad. 1867. *Ueber die Ausdrücke: altnordische, altnorwegische & isländische Sprache*.

Meissner, Rudolf. 1902. *Die Strengleikar: Ein Beitrag zur Geschichte der altnordischen Prosalitteratur*.

MHN = *Monumenta Historica Norvegiæ: Latinske kildeskrifter til Norges historie i middelalderen*. 1880. Ed. Gustav Storm. Reprinted 1973.

Moe, Moltke. 1925–27. *Samlede skrifter* I–III. Ed. Knut Liestøl.

Morkinskinna. 1932. Ed. Finnur Jónsson. Samfund til Udgivelse af gammel nordisk Litteratur LIII.

NgL = *Norges gamle Love indtil 1387* I–V. 1846–95. Ed. R. Keyser, P. A. Munch and G. Storm.

Njáls saga. In *Brennu-Njáls saga*. 1954. Ed. Einar Ól. Sveinsson. ÍF XII.

Noonan, Thomas S. 1986. 'Kievan Rus'. In *Dictionary of the Middle Ages* VII, 244–52.

Nordal, Sigurður. 1914. *Om Olaf den Helliges saga: En kritisk undersøgelse*.

Nordal, Sigurður. 1941. 'Gunnhildur konungamóðir', *Samtíð og saga* I, 135–55. Reprinted in *Áfangar* II, 1944, 249–73.

Noreen, Adolf. 1923. *Altisländische und altnorwegische grammatik (Laut- und flexionslehre)*. 4th ed.

Ó Corráin, D. 1972. *Ireland before the Normans.*
Oddr Snorrason. 1853. *Kong Olaf Tryggvesöns saga.* Ed. P. A. Munch.
Oddr Snorrason. 1932. *Saga Ólafs Tryggvasonar af Oddr Snorrason munk.* Ed. Finnur Jónsson.
Ólafía Einarsdóttir. 1964. *Studier i kronologisk metode i tidlig islandsk historieskrivning.*
Óláfs saga Tryggvasonar en mesta. 1958–61. Ed. Ólafur Halldórsson. Editiones Arnamagnæanæ A I–II.
Ólafur Halldórsson. 1969. 'Snjófríðar drápa'. In *Afmælisrit Jóns Helgasonar.* Ed. Jakob Benediktsson *et al.*, 147–59. Reprinted in *Grettisfærsla*, 1990, 217–30.
Ólafur Halldórsson. 1990. 'Eftirmáli'. In *Grettisfærsla*, 230–32.
Paasche, Fredrik. 1922. 'Tendens og syn i kongesagaen', *Edda* XVII, 1–17.
Paasche, Fredrik. 1957. *Norges og Islands litteratur inntil utgangen av middelalderen.* 2nd ed. revised by Anne Holtsmark.
Perkins, Richard. 1987. 'Steigar-Þórir's couplet and Steinn Herdísarson II: Notes and Queries', *Saga-Book* XXII:2, 109–115.
Pritsak, Omeljan. 1981. *The Origin of Rus'* I. *Old Scandinavian Sources other than the Sagas.*
Runciman, Stephen. 1951–54. *A History of the Crusades.*
Rygh, Oluf. 1897–1936. *Norske Gaardnavne.* Forord og indledning, I–XIX.
Rygh, Oluf. 1904. *Norske Elvenavne.*
Sawyer, Peter H. 1987. 'The process of Scandinavian Christianization in the tenth and eleventh centuries'. In *The Christianization of Scandinavia: Report of a Symposium held at Kungälv, Sweden, 4–9 August 1985.* Ed. Birgit Sawyer, Peter Sawyer and Ian Wood, 68–87.
Saxo Grammaticus. 1931. *Gesta Danorum.* Ed. J. Olrik and H. Raeder.
Schreiner, Johan. 1928. *Saga og oldfunn*: *Studier til Norges eldste historie.*
Seeberg, Axel. 1978–79. 'Five Kings', *Saga-Book* XX:1–2, 106–13.
Seip, Didrik Arup. 1938–39. 'Ágrip—Hryggjarstykki', *Arkiv för nordisk filologi* LIV, 238–39.
Seip, Didrik Arup. 1955. *Norsk språkhistorie til omkring 1370.*
Separate *Óláfs saga helga* = *Saga Óláfs konungs hins helga: Den store saga om Olav den hellige efter Pergamenthåndskrift i Kungliga Biblioteket i Stockholm nr. 2 4to, med varianter fra andre håndskrifter.* 1941. Ed. Oscar Albert Johnsen and Jón Helgason.

Bibliography 115

Skjd. = *Den norsk–islandske skjaldedigtning* A I–II B I–II. 1912–15. Ed. Finnur Jónsson.

SmhDmæ. = *Scriptores minores historiæ Danicæ medii ævi*. 1917–22. Ed. M. Cl. Gertz.

Sogner, Sølvi Bauge. 1961. 'Herse'. In *KLNM*, VI 512–13.

Stefán Karlsson. 1978. 'Om norvagismer i islandske håndskrifter', *Maal og minne*, 87–101.

Stefán Karlsson. 1979. 'Islandsk bogeksport til Norge i middelalderen', *Maal og minne*, 1–17.

Stenton, Frank M. 1971. *Anglo-Saxon England*. 3rd ed.

Storm, Gustav. 1871. 'Norske historieskrivere paa Kong Sverres tid', *Aarbøger for nordisk Oldkyndighed og Historie*, 410–31.

Storm, Gustav. 1873. *Snorre Sturlassöns historieskrivning: En kritisk undersögelse*.

Storm, Gustav. 1876. *De ældste Forbindelser mellem den norske og den islandske historiske Litteratur*.

Storm, Gustav (ed.). 1888. *Islandske Annaler indtil 1578*.

Storm, Gustav. 1893. 'Vore Forfædres Tro paa Sjælevandring og deres Opkaldelsessystem', *Arkiv för nordisk filologi* IX, 199–222.

Strömbäck, Dag. 1975. *The Conversion of Iceland: A Survey*. Trans. Peter Foote.

Sverris saga 1920 = *Sverris saga etter Cod. AM 327 4°*. Ed. Gustav Indrebø. Reprinted 1981.

Sørensen, Preben Meulengracht. 1980. *Norrønt nid*. English translation by Joan Turville-Petre, *The Unmanly Man: Concepts of Sexual Defamation in Early Northern Society*, 1983.

Theodoricus = *Theodorici Monachi Historia de Antiquitate Regum Norwagiensium*. In *MHN* 3–68.

Turville-Petre, E. O. G. 1951. *The Heroic Age of Scandinavia*.

Turville-Petre, E. O. G. 1953. *Origins of Icelandic Literature*.

Turville-Petre, E. O. G. 1964. *Myth and Religion of the North: The Religion of Ancient Scandinavia*.

Ulset, Tor. 1983. *Det genetiske forholdet mellom Ágrip, Historia Norwegiæ og Historia de antiquitate regum Norwagiensium*.

Vries, Jan de. 1964–67. *Altnordische Literaturgeschichte* I–II. 2nd ed.

Þorsteinn Vilhjálmsson. 1990. 'Raunvísindi á miðöldum'. In *Alþýðuvísindi*. Ed. Frosti F. Jóhannesson. Íslensk þjóðmenning VII, 1–50.

INDEX OF PERSONAL NAMES
(References are to the chapter numbers)

Aðalsteinn (Æthelstan), King of England 2, 5, 7
Álfífa (Ælfgifu), mistress of Knútr ríki 27, 32, 35
Ámundi Gyrðisson 60
Áslákr of Finneyjar 31
Áslákr Áskelsson, called 'Fitjaskalli' ('bald man of Fitjar') 26
Ástríðr (Estríð) Eiríksdóttir, mother of Óláfr Tryggvason 17
Ástríðr, daughter of Óláfr sœnski 25
Ástríðr, sister of Knútr ríki 37
Atli 35

Bergljót Þórisdóttir, mother of Hákon jarl 11
Bjaðmunjo Mýrjartaksdóttir (Biadmuin, daughter of Muirchertach) 51
Bjǫrn, called 'hinn digri' ('the stout') 31
Bjǫrn, son of Haraldr hárfagri, called 'kaupmaðr' ('merchant') or 'buna' ('club-foot'?) 2, 5, 23

Dagr Eilífsson 50, 60
Dagr, son of Haraldr hárfagri 2

Eggjar-Kálfr: see Kálfr Árnason of Egg
Egill Áskelsson of Forland 48
Einarr Eindriðason, called 'þambarskelmir' ('bowstring-shaker') 24, 34
Eiríkr Hákonarson, jarl, ruled Norway 1000–14, called 'inn ríki' ('the great') 13, 20, 21, 23
Eiríkr Haraldsson, King of Norway c.940–54, called 'blóðøx' ('blood-axe') 2, 5, 7
Erlendr Þorfinnsson, jarl in Orkney, father of St Magnús 50
Erlendr of Gerði 31
Erlingr, called 'inn gamli' ('the old') 9

Erlingr, son of Eiríkr blóðøx 5, 6
Erlingr Kyrpinga-Ormsson, jarl, called 'inn skakki' ('the crooked') 60
Erlingr Skjálgsson of Sóli 26
Estríð: see Ástríðr Eiríksdóttir
Eysteinn Erlendsson, archbishop 42
Eysteinn, son of Haraldr gilli, King of Norway 1142–57 (with his brothers Ingi and Sigurðr) 60
Eysteinn, son of Haraldr hárfagri 2
Eysteinn, son of Magnús berleggr, King of Norway 1103–22 (with his brothers Sigurðr and Óláfr) 48, 52, 55
Eyvindr, son of Eiríkr blóðøx 5
Eyvindr Finnsson 51
Eyvindr Finnsson, called 'skáldaspillir' ('plagiarist'?) 6, 15
Eyvindr Ǫzurarson, called 'skreyja' ('braggart'?) 6

Fiðr (Finnr) Árnason 41
Fróði, son of Haraldr hárfagri 2

Gamli, son of Eiríkr blóðøx 5, 6, 23
Geirsteinn 60
Goðormr, son of Eiríkr blóðøx 5
Goðormr, son of Haraldr hárfagri 2
Goðrøðr = Guðrøðr
Gormr, son of Eiríkr blóðøx 5, 6
Gregóríús Dagsson 50
Guðrún, called 'Lundasól' ('sun of Lundir') 13
Guðrøðr Bjarnason, grandfather of Óláfr helgi 23
Guðrøðr, son of Eiríkr blóðøx, called 'ljómi' ('lustre') 5, 8
Guðrøðr, son of Haraldr hárfagri, called 'ljómi' ('lustre') 2
Guðrøðr, son of Haraldr hárfagri, called 'skirja' ('cow'?) 2

Index of personal names

Gull-Haraldr: see Haraldr Knútsson
Gunnhildr, daughter of Óláfr helgi 25
Gunnhildr Ǫzurardóttir, called 'konungamóðir' ('mother of kings') 5–7, 11, 16, 17
Gunnrøðr, son of Haraldr hárfagri 2
Guthormr = Goðormr
Gyða Skoptadóttir 60
Gyrðr 60
Gyrðr Bárðarson, called 'Sáða-Gyrðr' 60

Hákon Eiríksson, jarl 21, 23, 27
Hákon, son of Haraldr hárfagri, king of Norway c.954–65, called 'Aðalsteinsfóstri' ('Æthelstan's fosterling') or 'inn góði' ('the good') 2, 5, 6, 8
Hákon Magnússon, King of Norway 1093–94 (with Magnús berleggr), known as '(Steigar-)Þórisfóstri' ('Steigar-Þórir's fosterling') 43, 46–48
Hákon Sigurðarson, jarl, ruled Norway 975–95, called 'inn ríki' ('the great'); also 'inn illi' (the bad') 10–14, 16, 17, 19–21
Hálfdan, son of Eiríkr blóðøx 5
Hálfdan Guðrøðarson, called 'inn svarti' ('the black') 1, 2
Hálfdan, son of Haraldr hárfagri, called 'hvítbeinn' ('white-leg') or 'háfœta' ('high-leg') 2
Hálfdan, son of Haraldr hárfagri, called 'inn svarti' ('the black') 2
Hálfdan, son of Sigurðr hrísi, called 'hvítbeinn' ('white-leg') or 'heikilnefr' ('pointy-nose'?) 39
Halldórr of Skerðingssteðja 13
Hár(r) (Óðinn) 1
Haraldr Eiríksson, king of Norway c.965–75, called 'gráfeldr' ('grey-cloak') 5, 6, 8–12
Haraldr 'flettir' ('plunderer'?) 48
Haraldr Goðinason (Harold Godwineson), King of England 42
Haraldr Gormsson, King of Denmark, called 'blátǫnn' ('blue-tooth') 7, 10, 11
Haraldr Guðrøðarson, called 'inn grœnski' ('from Grenland'), father of Óláfr helgi 22, 23
Haraldr Hálfdanarson, king of Norway c.880–940, called 'hárfagri' ('fine-hair') 1–3, 5, 11, 16, 23, 39, 42
Haraldr Knútsson, called 'Gull-Haraldr' ('gold-Haraldr') 10
Haraldr, son of Magnús berleggr, King of Norway (with Magnús blindi) 1130–36, called 'gillikrist' or 'gilli' ('servant of Christ') 58, 59
Haraldr Sigurðarson, King of Norway 1046–66, called 'harðráði' ('hard-ruler') 31, 33, 39–43, 45, 48, 51
Hersir, king in Naumudal, ancestor of Hákon jarl 15
Hísingr Geirsteinsson 60
Hjarrandi Geirsteinsson 60
Hringr, son of Haraldr hárfagri 2
Hrœrekr, son of Haraldr hárfagri 2
Hugi, count, called 'inn digri' ('the stout') (Hugh, son of Richard, Viscount of Avranches) 50
Hǫkon = Hákon
Hǫrða-Knútr: see Knútr, son of Knútr ríki

Ingi, son of Haraldr gilli, King of Norway (with his brothers Sigurðr and Eysteinn) 1136–61, called 'krókhryggr' ('hunchback') 60
Ingi Steinkelsson, King of Sweden 49
Ingibjǫrg Ǫgmundardóttir, wife of Egill Áskelsson 48
Ingigerðr, daughter of King Óláfr Eiríksson of Sweden 25, 34
Ingiríðr Rǫgnvaldsdóttir 60

Jaritláfr Valdamarsson (Yaroslav), King of Russia 25, 34
Jólnir (Óðinn) 1

Kálfr Árnason of Egg 26, 31, 34
Karkr, thrall 13
Knútr Gormsson 10
Knútr, son of Knútr ríki, called 'Hǫrða-Knútr' 36
Knútr Sveinsson, called 'inn ríki' ('the great') 21, 26, 27, 36, 37
Kyrpinga-Ormr: see Ormr Sveinsson

Magnús Erlendsson, jarl in Orkney, saint 50
Magnús Óláfsson, King of Norway (with Hákon Magnússon) 1093–1103, called 'berleggr' or 'berfœttr' ('bare-leg') 46, 48–53, 58
Magnús, son of Óláfr helgi, King of Norway 1035–47, called 'inn góði' ('the good') 26, 34–40, 42, 48
Magnús, son of Sigurðr Jórsalafari, King of Norway (with Haraldr gilli) 1130–35, called 'inn blindi' ('the blind') 57–59
Magnús, son of Haraldr harðráði, King of Norway 1066–69 (with his brother Óláfr) 43, 45
Margrét, daughter of King Ingi of Sweden, married to Magnús berleggr 49
Mýrjartak Kondjálvason (Muirchertach Úa Briain), King of Munster 51
Mǫgnús = Magnús

Nikulaus Sigurðarson (or Skjaldvarar-son) 50

Óðinn 1
Óláfr Eiríksson, King of Sweden, called 'inn sœnski' ('the Swede') 13, 20, 25
Óláfr Haraldsson, King of Norway 1014–28, called 'inn digri' ('the stout') and, following his death, 'inn helgi' ('the saint') 22–26, 31–35, 38, 39, 44, 54
Óláfr, son of Haraldr harðráði, King of Norway 1066–93, called 'inn kyrri' ('the peaceful') or 'búandi' ('farmer') 42–44
Óláfr, son of Haraldr hárfagri, called 'digrbeinn' ('stout-leg') 2, 5, 16
Óláfr, son of Magnús berleggr, King of Norway 1103–15 (with his brothers Eysteinn and Sigurðr) 52, 55
Óláfr Tryggvason, King of Norway 995–1000 9, 13, 16, 17, 19–22
Ólof Haraldsdóttir 11
Ormr Sveinsson, called 'Kyrpinga-Ormr' 60
Óttarr, called 'birtingr' ('bright' or 'trout'?) 60
Ottó (Ordulf), Duke of Saxony 25

Páll (Póll) Þorfinnsson, jarl in Orkney 42

Ragnfrøðr, son of Eiríkr blóðøx 5, 8
Ragnhildr Skoptadóttir, sister of Gyða 60
Rǫgnvaldr Brúsason 31, 34
Rǫgnvaldr (Ragnarr), son of Haraldr hárfagri, called 'reykill' ('puller'?) 2
Rǫgnvaldr, son of Haraldr hárfagri 2

Sáða-Gyrðr: see Gyrðr Bárðarson
Sighvatr Þórðarson, poet 32, 35
Sigtryggr, son of Haraldr hárfagri 2
Sigurðr, bishop 19
Sigurðr, son of Eiríkr blóðøx, called 'slefa' ('drool' or 'snake'?) 5, 8, 9
Sigurðr, son of Hákon gamli, called 'Hyrnajarl' ('jarl of Yrjar': Hyrna- is probably for Yrna-, gen. pl. either of Yrjar, mod. Ørland, in Norðmœrr, or of Yrji, otherwise unattested, 'an inhabitant of Yrjar') 11

Index of personal names

Sigurðr Hálfdanarson, called 'sýr' (probably 'sow') 24, 39
Sigurðr, son of Haraldr gilli, King of Norway (with his brothers Ingi and Eysteinn) 1136–55, called 'munnr' ('mouth') 60
Sigurðr, son of Haraldr hárfagri, called 'hrísi' ('bastard'?) 2, 39
Sigurðr Hranason 50
Sigurðr, son of Magnús berleggr, King of Norway (with his brothers Eysteinn and Óláfr) 1103–30, called 'Jórsalafari' ('crusader') 29, 51–53, 55, 56, 58
Sigurðr Sigurðarson 50
Sigurðr, called 'ullstrengr' ('woolband') 48, 50
Skeiðar-Brandr 2
Skopti Ǫgmundarson 48
Snjófríðr Svásadóttir 2, 3
Steigar-Þórir: see Þórir Þórðarson
Svási, King of the Lapps 2, 3
Sveinn Álfífuson, son of Knútr ríki, King of Norway 1030–35 27, 32, 35, 36
Sveinn, called 'bryggjufótr' ('pierfoot'?) 34
Sveinn Hákonarson, jarl 13, 21, 23, 24
Sveinn Haraldsson, King of Denmark, called 'tjúguskegg' ('fork-beard') 20, 21
Sveinn, son of Haraldr flettir 48
Sveinn Úlfsson, King of Denmark 37, 38, 40, 41
Sygurðr = Sigurðr

Tósti Goðinason (Tostig Godwineson) 42
Tryggvi, son of Haraldr hárfagri 2
Tryggvi Óláfsson, King of Norway 9, 16, 17

Úlfr Hranason 50
Úlfr Óspaksson, 'stalleri' ('marshal') 39
Úlfr Þorgilsson, father of Sveinn, King of Denmark 37
Ulli (Erlendr), son of Hákon jarl 13

Vémundr, called 'vǫlubrjótr' ('breaker of sorceresses' or 'knuckle-crusher'?) 9
Víðkuðr (-kunnr) Jóansson 50, 51
Viðrir (Óðinn) 1
Vigða, wife of Hersir 15

Þangbrandr, priest 19
Þjóstólfr Álason 60
Þóra, mother of Hákon góði, called 'Mostrstǫng' ('pole of Mostr') 6
Þóra of Remol, mistress of Hákon jarl 13
Þórálfr Skólmsson, an Icelander, called 'inn sterki' ('the strong') 6
Þórir, brother of Magnús góði 40
Þórir Rǫgnvaldsson, jarl of Mœrr, called 'þegjandi' ('the silent') 11
Þórir Þórðarson, called 'Steigar-Þórir' 43, 46, 48
Þórir Þórisson, called 'hundr' ('dog') 26, 31
Þorkell, called 'klyppr' ('squarely-built'?) 9
Þorleifr Hǫrða-Kárason, called 'inn spaki' ('the wise') 4, 5
Þormóðr, priest 19
Þórólfr, called 'lúsa(r)skegg' ('lousebeard') 9, 17, 18
Þorsteinn, called 'knarrasmiðr' ('boatbuilder') 31
Þriði (Óðinn) 1
Þyri, daughter of Haraldr blátǫnn 20

Ǫgmundr, son of Kyrpinga-Ormr, called 'dengir' ('hammerer'?) 60
Ǫgmundr Skoptason 50
Ǫgmundr, called 'sviptir' ('depriver', 'pirate'?) 60
Ǫmundi = Ámundi
Ǫzurr, father of Gunnhildur konungamóðir, called 'lafskegg' ('danglingbeard') or 'toti' ('teat') 5

INDEX OF PLACE-NAMES
(References are to the chapter numbers)

Alreksstaðir (Årstad), Hǫrðaland 6, 9
Austrvegr, Austrvegir (eastern Europe, Russia etc.) 25, 26, 33, 34, 39

Borgund, Sunnmœrr 26
Brenneyjar, islands near the mouth of the Gautelfr, Sweden 36
Bretland (Britain; Wales) 50
Byskupssteinn, Fitjar, Hǫrðaland 6

Dalr [= Sunndalr (Sundal) and Norðdalr (Nordal)], Sweden 49
Danmǫrk (Denmark) 2, 5, 7, 11, 20, 24, 35–38, 40, 41, 48, 55

Egg (Egge), Sparbyggvafylki, Þrándheimr 26
Eistland (Estonia) 18
Elgjusetr [= Elgisetr] (Elgeseter), Niðaróss 42
England 2, 5–7, 13, 19, 21–23, 26, 36, 37, 42, 51–53
Englandshaf (North Sea) 27
Eysýsla (Ösel/Saaremaa), Eistland 17
Eyrar (Ørene), in Niðaróss 46

Finney(jar) (Finnøy), Rogaland 31
Fitjar (Fitje), Storð, Hǫrðaland 6
Flæmingjaland (Flanders) 19
Forland (Folland), Norðmœrr 48
Fræði (Frædøy/Frei), Norðmœrr 5
Færeyjar (The Faeroes) 19

Gamlaleir, Gaulardalr 5
Garðar [= Garðaríki, Russia] 24
Garðr [= Mikligarðr] 39
Gauladalr, Gaulardalr (Gauldalen), Þrándheimr 5, 13
Gautland [i. e. Vestra-Gautland] (Götaland) 5, 49

Gerði (Gjerde), Hǫrðaland 31
Grenmarr (Langesundsfjorden), Grenland 24
Gulaþingslǫg, Golaþingslǫg, district in western Norway 46

Haðaland (Hadeland), Upplǫnd 1, 2
Hafrsvágr [= Hafrsfjǫrðr (Hasfjord, Hafrsfjorden)], Rogaland 2
Hákonarhella (Håkonshella), Hǫrðaland 6
Halland, Sweden 41
Hallvarðskirkja, Oslo 58
Hálogaland (Hålogaland) 48
Háls í Limafirði, Denmark 10, 12
Harmr (Velfjorden), Hálogaland 48
Hasleyjarsund, Rogaland 4
Haugar (Haugesund), Rogaland 4
Haukbœr (Håkeby), Ranríki 45
Hefring (Høvringen), near Niðaróss 46, 48
Helganes (Helgenæs), Jótland 37
Hesjutún (Hesstun), Hálogaland 48
Hjaltland (Shetland) 19
Hlýrskógsheiðr (Lyrskovshede), Denmark (but now in Germany) 38
Hólmgarðr (Novgorod) 17, 18
Hólmr [= Niðarhólmr], Niðaróss 13
Hringaríki (Ringerike), Upplǫnd 1
Hǫkló [= Ǫgló; cf. Rygh 1897–1936, XV 29] (Skatval), Stjórdœlafylki, Þrándheimr 10
Hǫrðaland (Hordaland) 19

Írland (Ireland) 19, 51, 58
Ísland (Iceland) 19, 29

Jaðarr (Jæren), Rygjafylki 2
Jamtaland (Jämtland), Sweden 31
Jarlshellir (Jarlshelleren), Gaulardalr 13

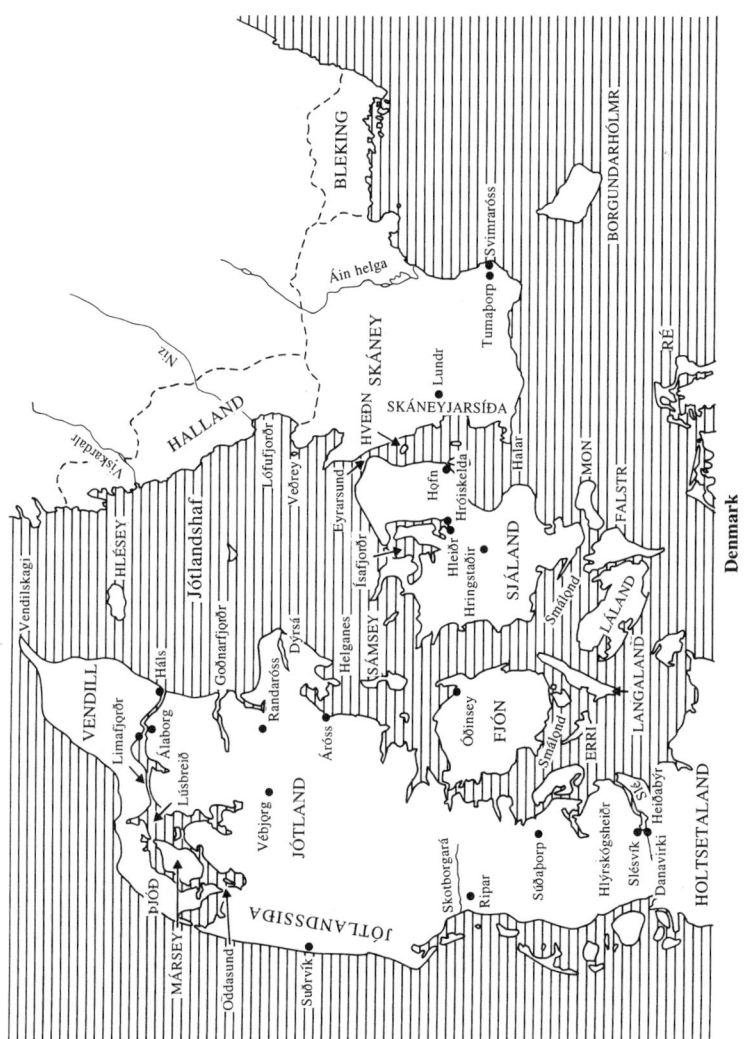

Denmark

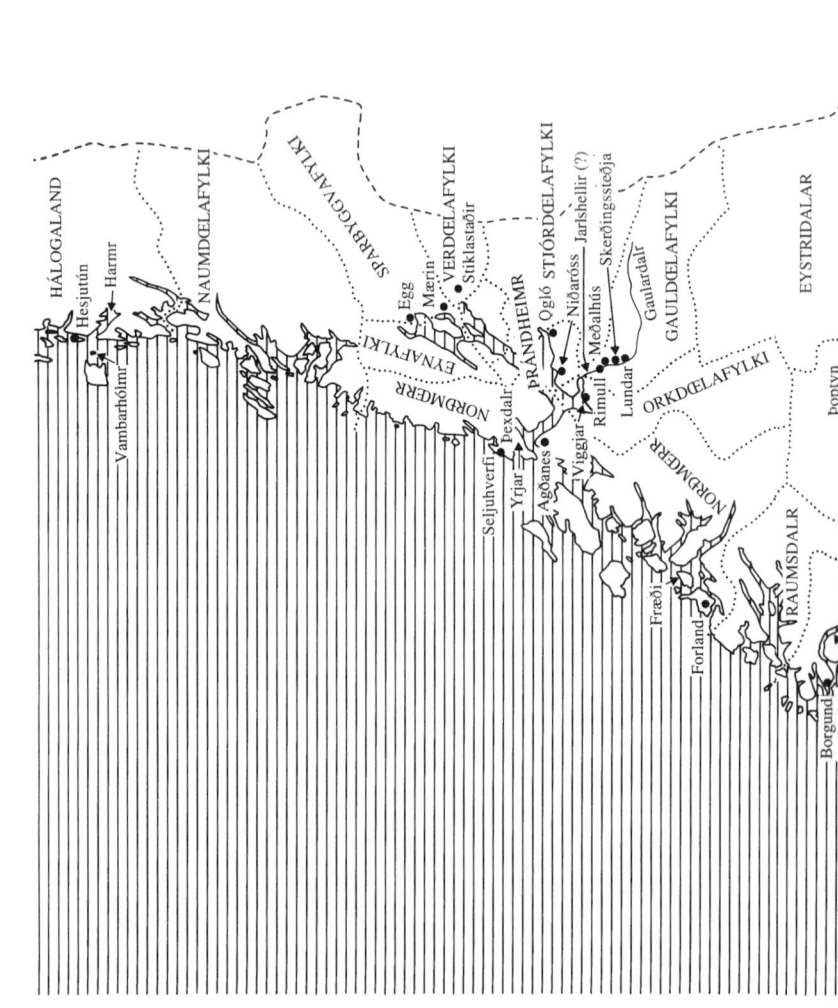

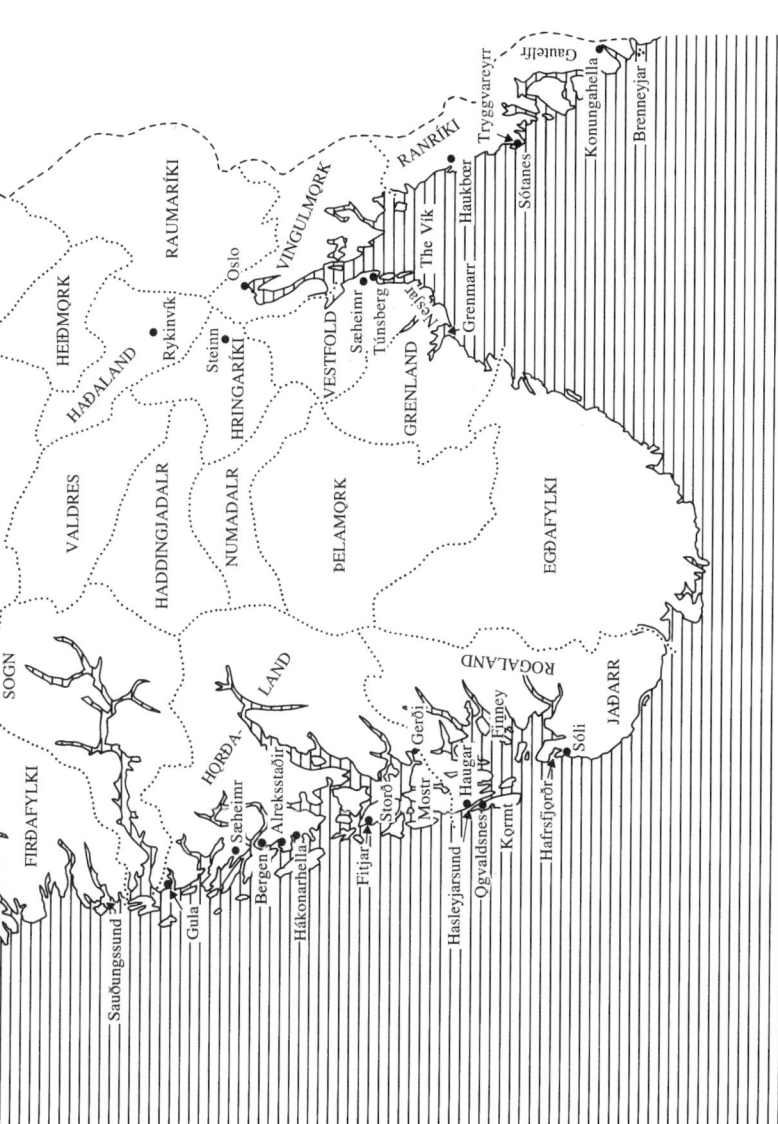

Central and South Norway

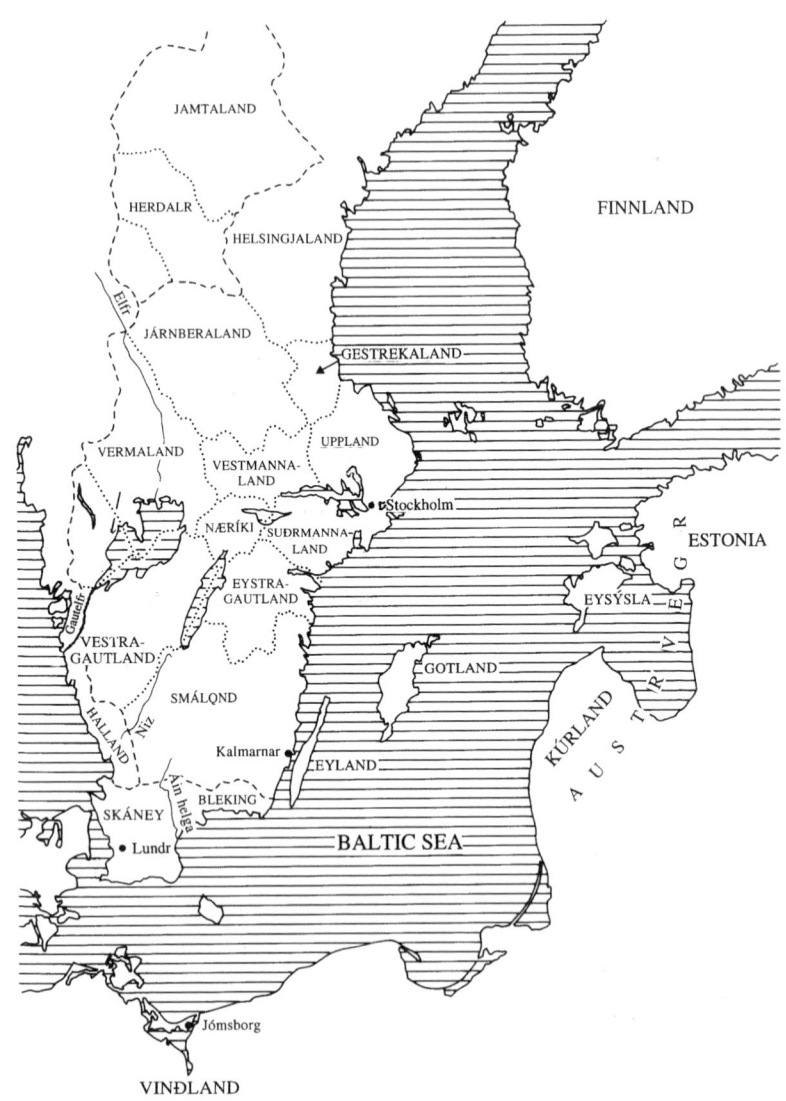

Sweden and the Baltic

Index of place-names

Jómsborg (possibly Wolin in present-day Poland) 19
Jórsalaland (The Holy Land) 20
Jórsalir (Jerusalem) 52, 53

Kalmarnar (Kalmar), Smálǫnd, Sweden 56
Kaupangr [= Niðaróss] 13, 46–48, 52
Klémetskirkja, Niðaróss 46
Kristskirkja, Niðaróss 40, 47, 52
Kǫrmt (Karmøy), Rogaland 5

Limafjǫrðr (Limfjorden), Denmark 10, 12
Lundar (Lunde), Gaulardalr 13

Máríukirkja, Niðaróss 42
Meðalhús (Melhus), Gaulardalr 13
Mikligarðr (Constantinople or Byzantium) 33, 55
Mo(r)str (Moster), Hǫrðaland 6, 19
Mærin (Mære), Sparbyggvafylki, Þrándheimr 5
Mœrr (Møre) 11

Naumudalr (Namdalen) 15
Nesjar (Brunlanes), Vestfold 24
Niðaróss (Trondheim), Strindafylki, Þrándheimr 35, 42, 44–46
Niz (Nissan), river in Halland, Sweden 41
Norðhǫrðaland (Nordhordland) 6
Norðimbraland (Northumbria) 7, 42
Nóregr (Norway) 2, 4–6, 8–11, 13, 14, 16, 17, 19, 21, 23–26, 33, 36, 39–43, 45, 49, 55, 57, 58
Normandie (Normandy) 42

Orkneyjar (Orkney) 17, 19, 42, 50
Oslo, Ǫsló (Oslo), Vingulmǫrk 58

Pétrskirkja (St Peter's), Mikligarðr 55

Ranríki (Bohuslän), Sweden 41, 45

Raumaríki (Romerike) 16
Raumsdalr (Romsdal) 48
Remol [= Rimul(l)] (Romol), Gaulardalr 13
Rogaland 4
Rykinvík (Røykenvik), Rǫnd 1
Rǫnd (Randsfjorden), lake in Haðaland, Upplǫnd 1

Sauðungasund (Sauesundet), Fjalir, Firðafylki 23
Saxland (Saxony) 25, 55
Seljuhverfi (Jøssund), Norðmœrr 48
Selund [older form of Sjóland] 5
Sjóland, Sjáland (Sjælland, Zealand), Denmark 20, 40
Skáney (Skåne) 5
Skerðingssteðja (Skjerdingstad), Gaulardalr 13
Skotborgará (Kongeå), Jótland 38
Skotland (Scotland) 19, 50
Skúlagarðr, Niðaróss 46
Sleygsarfjǫrðr (Storfjorden), Sunnmœrr 26
Smálǫnd (Småland), Sweden 56
Sóli (Sola), Jaðarr, Rygjafylki 26
Sótanes (Sotenäs), Ranríki 16
Spánialand (Spain) 7
Steinbjǫrg (Steinberget), near Niðaróss 13, 47
Steinn (Stein), Hringaríki, Upplǫnd 1
Stiklastaðir (Stiklestad), Veradalr, Þrándheimr 31
Storð (Stord), Hǫrðaland 6
Suðreyjar (Hebrides) 23
Sunnmœrr (Sunnmøre) 48
Súrnadalr (Surnadal), Norðmœrr 5
Svíþjóð (Sweden) 13, 17, 31, 36
Sæheimr (Seim), Hǫrðaland 6
Sæheimr (Jarlsberg?), Vestfold 58
Sæla [= Selja] (Selje), Firðir 23

Tryggvareyrr, Sótanes, Ranríki 16
Túnsberg (Tønsberg), Vestfold 58

Úlaðsstír (Ulster), Ireland 51
Ungeraland (Hungary) 55
Upplǫnd (Oppland) 17, 24, 48

Vagnvíkastrǫnd (Vanvikan), Þrándheimr 48
Valdalr (Valldal), Sunnmœrr 26
Vambarhólmr (Vomba), Hálogaland 48
Varðynjar (Valbo), Sweden 49
Véar (Vedbo), Sweden 49
Veradalr (Verdal), Þrándheimr 31
Vestrlǫnd 7
Vigða, Naumudalr 15
Vigg (Viggja), Orkadalr, Þrándheimr 48
Vík [= Víkin] 47, 60
Vinðland, Vinnland, Vennland, Vendland (Wendland, Land of the Wends; in modern Poland and northern Germany) 2, 19, 20, 37
Vǫrðynjar = Varðynjar

Þexdalr (Teksdal), Seljuhverfi, Norðmœrr 48
Þoptyn [= Þoptar] (Tofte), Guðbrandsdalar 3
Þrándheimr, Þrǫndheimr (Trondheim(en)/Trøndelag) 5, 10, 31, 40, 48

Ǫgló (Skatval), Stjórdœlafylki, Þrándheimr 10
Ǫgvaldsnes (Avaldsnes), Kǫrmt, Rygjafylki 5
Ǫsló = Oslo

INDEX OF OTHER NAMES
(References are to the chapter numbers)

Barthólómeúsmessa 51
Danir (Danes) 10, 18
Eistr (Estonians) 17
Gautar (people of Götaland (southern Sweden)) 18
Golaþingslǫg (the law of Gulaþing in western Norway) 5
Háleygir (people of Hálogaland) 11
Háleygjatal, a poem by Eyvindr skáldaspillir 15
Írir (Irishmen) 51
Jóansmessa 19
Kvernbiti, a sword 6

Míkjálsmessa 19
Miklagildi 44
Mœrir (people of Mœrr) 11
Norðmenn (Norwegians) 6, 8, 18, 28
Oddmjór, a poem 2
Ormr inn langi, a ship 20
Upplendingar (people of Upplǫnd, Norway) 46
Vǫrsar (people of Vǫrs, modern Voss, Hǫrðaland) 9
Þrœndir (people of Þrándheimr) 5, 31, 35, 46